AN ADVENTURE
WITH A GENIUS

Recollections of JOSEPH PULITZER.

ALLEYNE IRELAND

1st WORLD
LIBRARY
Literary Society

An Adventure With A Genius

Alleyne Ireland

© 1st World Library, 2006
PO Box 2211
Fairfield, IA 52556
www.1stworldlibrary.com
First Edition

LCCN: 2006907697

Softcover ISBN: 1-4218-2415-9
Hardcover ISBN: 1-4218-2315-2
eBook ISBN: 1-4218-2515-5

Purchase *"An Adventure With A Genius"*
as a traditional bound book at:
www.1stWorldLibrary.com/purchase.asp?ISBN=1-4218-2415-9

1st World Library is a literary, educational organization
dedicated to:

- Creating a free internet library of downloadable ebooks

- Hosting writing competitions and offering book
publishing scholarships.

Interested in more 1st World Library books?
contact: literacy@1stworldlibrary.com
Check us out at: www.1stworldlibrary.com

1st World Library Literary Society

Giving Back to the World

"If you want to work on the core problem, it's early school literacy."

- James Barksdale, former CEO of Netscape

"No skill is more crucial to the future of a child, or to a democratic and prosperous society, than literacy."

- Los Angeles Times

Literacy... means far more than learning how to read and write... The aim is to transmit... knowledge and promote social participation."

- UNESCO

"Literacy is not a luxury, it is a right and a responsibility. If our world is to meet the challenges of the twenty-first century we must harness the energy and creativity of all our citizens."

- President Bill Clinton

"Parents should be encouraged to read to their children, and teachers should be equipped with all available techniques for teaching literacy, so the varying needs and capacities of individual kids can be taken into account."

- Hugh Mackay

DEDICATED
BY KIND PERMISSION
AND
WITH SINCERE REGARD
TO
MRS. JOSEPH PULITZER

PREFACE

In the course of my wanderings about the labyrinth of life it has been my good fortune to find awaiting me around every corner some new adventure. If these have generally lacked that vividness of action which to the eye of youth is the very test of adventure, they have been rich in a kind of experience which to a mature and reflective mind has a value not to be measured in terms of dramatic incident.

My adventures, in a word, have been chiefly those of personal contact with the sort of men whose lives are the material around which history builds its story, and from which fiction derives all that lends to it the air of reality.

I have had friends and acquaintances in a score of countries, and in every station of society - kings and beggars, viceroys and ward- politicians, judges and criminals, men of brain and men of brawn.

My first outstanding adventure was with a stern and formidable man, the captain of a sailing vessel, of whose ship's company I was one in a voyage across the Pacific; one of my most recent was with a man not less stern or formidable, with the man who is the central figure in the present narrative.

The tale has been told before in a volume entitled "Joseph Pulitzer: Reminiscences of a Secretary." The volume has been out of print for some time, but the continued demand for it has called for its re-issue. The change in title has been made in response to many suggestions that the character of the material is more aptly described as "An Adventure with a Genius."

ALLEYNE IRELAND.
New York, 1920.

CONTENTS

CHAPTER I

IN A CASTING NET

A long illness, a longer convalescence, a positive injunction from my doctor to leave friends and business associates and to seek some spot where a comfortable bed and good food could be had in convenient proximity to varied but mild forms of amusement - and I found myself in the autumn of the year 1910 free and alone in the delightful city of Hamburg.

All my plans had gone down wind, and as I sat at my table in the Café Ziechen, whence, against the background of the glittering blue of the Alster, I could see the busy life of the Alter Jungfernstieg and the Alsterdamm, my thoughts turned naturally to the future.

It is not the easiest thing in the world to reconstruct at forty years of age the whole scheme of your life; but my illness, and other happenings of a highly disagreeable character, had compelled me to abandon a career to which I had devoted twenty years of arduous labor; and the question which pressed for an immediate answer was: What are you going to do now?

Various alternatives presented themselves. There had been a suggestion that I should take the editorship of a newspaper in Calcutta; an important financial house in London had offered me the direction of its interests in Western Canada; a post in the service of the Government of India had been mentioned as a possibility by certain persons in authority.

My own inclination, the child of a weary spirit and of the lassitude of ill health, swayed me in the direction of a quiet retreat in Barbados, that peaceful island of an eternal summer cooled by the northeast trades, where the rush and turmoil of modern life are unknown and where a very modest income more than suffices for all the needs of a simple existence.

I shall never know to what issue my reflections upon these matters would have led me, for a circumstance, in the last degree trivial, intervened to turn my thoughts into an entirely new channel, and to guide me, though I could not know it at the time, into the service of Joseph Pulitzer.

My waiter was extremely busy serving a large party of artillery officers at an adjoining table. I glanced through The Times and the Hamburger Nachrichten, looked out for a while upon the crowded street, and then, resigning myself to the delay in getting my lunch, picked up The Times again and did what I had never done before in my life - read the advertisements under the head "Professional Situations."

All except one were of the usual type, the kind in which a prospective employer flatters a prospective employee by classing as "professional" the services of a typewriter or of a companion to an elderly gentleman who resides within easy distance of an important provincial town.

One advertisement, however, stood out from the rest on account of the peculiar requirements set forth in its terse appeal. It ran something after this fashion: "Wanted, an intelligent man of about middle age, widely read, widely traveled, a good sailor, as companion-secretary to a gentleman. Must be prepared to live abroad. Good salary. Apply, etc."

My curiosity was aroused; and at first sight I appeared to meet the requirements in a reasonable measure. I had certainly traveled widely, and I was an excellent sailor - excellent to the point of offensiveness. Upon an unfavorable construction I could claim to be middle-aged at forty; and I was prepared to live abroad in the unlikely event of any one fixing upon a country which could be properly called "abroad" from the standpoint of a man who had not spent twelve consecutive months in any place since he was fifteen years old.

As for intelligence, I reflected that for ninety-nine people out of a hundred intelligence in others means no more than the discovery of a person who is in intellectual acquiescence with themselves, and that if the necessity arose I could probably affect an acquiescence which would serve all the purposes of a fundamental identity of convictions.

Two things, however, suggested possible difficulties, the questions of what interpretations the advertiser placed upon the terms "widely read" and "good salary." I could not claim to be widely read in any conventional sense, for I was not a university graduate, and the very extensive reading I had done in my special line of study - the control and development of tropical dependencies - though it might entitle me to some consideration as a student in that field had left me woefully ignorant of general literature. Would the ability to discuss with intelligence the Bengal Regulation of 1818, or the British Guiana Immigration Ordinance of 1891 be welcomed as a set-off to a complete unfamiliarity with Milton's "Comus" and Gladstone's essay on the epithets of motion in Homer?

On the subject of what constituted a "good salary" experience had taught me to expect a very wide divergence of view, not only along the natural line of cleavage between the person paying and the person receiving the salary, but also between one employer and another and between one employee and another; and I recalled a story, told me in my infancy, in which a certain British laboring man had been heard to remark that he would not be the Czar of Russia, no, not for thirty shillings a week. But that element in the situation might, I reflected, very well be left to take care of itself.

I finished my lunch, and then replied to the advertisement, giving my English address. My letter, a composition bred of the conflicting influences of pride, modesty, prudence, and curiosity, brought forth in due course a brief reply in which I was bidden to an interview in that part of London where fashion and business prosperity seek to ape each other.

Upon presenting myself at the appointed hour I was confronted by a gentleman whose severity of manner I learned later to recognize as the useful mask to a singularly genial and kindly nature.

Our interview was long and, to me at any rate, rather embarrassing, since it resolved itself into a searching cross-examination by a past-master in the art. Who were my parents? When and where had I been born? Where had I been educated? What were my means of livelihood? What positions had I filled since I went out into the world? What countries had I visited? What books had I read? What books had I written? To what magazines and reviews had I contributed? Who were my friends? Was I fond of music, of painting, of the drama? Had I a sense of humor? Had I a good temper or a good control of a bad one? What languages could I speak or read? Did I enjoy good health? Was I of a nervous disposition? Had I tact and discretion? Was I a good horseman, a good sailor, a good talker, a good reader?

When it came to asking me whether I was a good horseman AND a good sailor, I realized that anyone who expected to find these two qualities combined in one man was quite capable of demanding that his companion-secretary should be able to knit woollen socks, write devotional verse, and compute the phases of the moon.

I remember chuckling to myself over this quaint conceit; I was to learn later that it came unpleasantly near the truth.

Under this close examination I felt that I had made rather a poor showing. This was due in some measure, no doubt, to the fact that my questioner abruptly left any topic as soon as he discovered that I knew something about it, and began to angle around, with disturbing success, to find the things I did not know about.

At one point, however, I scored a hit. After I had been put through my paces, a process which seemed to me to end only at the exact point where my questioner could no longer remember the name of anything in the universe about which he could frame an interrogation, it was my turn to ask questions.

Was the person I was addressing the gentleman who needed the companion?

No, he was merely his agent. As a matter of fact the person on whose behalf he was acting was an American.

I nodded in a non-committal way.

He was also a millionaire.

I bowed the kind of bow that a Frenchman makes when he says Mais parfaitement.

Furthermore he was totally blind.

"Joseph Pulitzer," I said.

"How in the world did you guess that?" asked my companion.

"That wasn't a guess," I replied. "You advertised for an intelligent man; and this is simply where my intelligence commences to show itself. An intelligent man couldn't live as long as I have in the United States without hearing a good deal about Joseph Pulitzer; and, after all, the country isn't absolutely overrun with blind millionaires."

At the close of the interview I was told that I would be reported upon. In the meantime would I kindly send in a written account of the interview, in the fullest possible detail, as a test of my memory, sense of accuracy, and literary style.

Nor was this all. As I prepared to take my departure I was handed the address of another gentleman who would also examine me and make a report. Before I got out of the room my inquisitor said, "It may interest you to know that we have had more than six hundred applications for the post, and that it may, therefore, take some time before the matter is definitely settled."

I was appalled. Evidently I had been wasting my time, for I could have no doubt that the gallant six hundred would include a sample of every kind of pundit, stationary or vagrant, encompassed within the seven seas; and against such competition I felt my chances to be just precisely nothing.

My companion observed my discomfiture. and as he shook hands he said, "Oh, that doesn't really mean very much. As a matter of fact we were able to throw out more than five hundred and fifty applications merely for self-evident reasons. A number of school teachers and bank clerks applied, and in general these gentlemen said that although they had not traveled they would have no objection to living abroad, and that they might venture to hope that if they DID go to sea they would prove to be good sailors.

"Most of them appeared to think that the circumstance of being middle-aged would off-set their deficiencies in other directions. There are really only a few gentlemen whom we can consider as being likely to meet Mr. Pulitzer's requirements, and the selection will be made finally by Mr. Pulitzer himself. It is very probable that you will be asked to go to Mentone to spend a fortnight or so on Mr. Pulitzer's yacht or at his villa at Cap Martin, as he never engages anybody until he has had the candidate with him for a short visit.

"And, by the way, would you mind writing a short narrative of your life, not more than two thousand words? It would interest Mr. Pulitzer and would help him to reach a decision in your case. You might also send me copies of some of your writings."

Thus ended my interview with Mr. James M. Tuohy, the London correspondent of the New York World.

My next step was to call upon the second inquisitor, Mr. George Ledlie. I found him comfortably installed at an hotel in the West End. He was an American, very courteous and pleasant, but evidently prepared to use a probe without any consideration for the feelings of the victim.

As my business was to reveal myself, I wasted no time, and for about an hour I rambled along on the subject of my American experiences. I do not know to this day what sort of an impression I created upon this gentleman, but I felt at the time that it ought to have been a favorable one.

We had many friends in common; I had recently been offered a lectureship in the university from which he had graduated; some of my books had been published in America by firms in whose standing he had confidence; I paraded a slight acquaintance with three Presidents of the United States, and produced from my pocketbook letters from two of them; we found that we were both respectful admirers of a charming lady who had recently undergone a surgical operation; he had been a guest at my club in Boston, I had been a guest at his club in New York. When I left him I thought poorly of the chances of the remnant of the six hundred.

Some weeks passed and I heard nothing more of the matter. During this time I had leisure to think over what I had heard from time to time about Joseph Pulitzer, and to speculate, with the aid of some imaginative friends, upon the probable advantages and disadvantages of the position for which I was a candidate.

Gathered together, my second-hand impressions of Joseph Pulitzer made little more than a hazy outline. I had heard or read that he had landed in New York in the early sixties, a penniless youth unable to speak a word of English; that after a remarkable series of adventures he had become a newspaper proprietor and, later, a millionaire; that he had been stricken blind at the height of his career; that his friends and his enemies agreed in describing him as a man of extraordinary ability and of remarkable character; that he had been victorious in a bitter controversy with President Roosevelt; that one of the Rothschilds had remarked that if Joseph Pulitzer had not lost his eyesight and his health he, Pulitzer, would have collected into his hands all the money there was; that he was the subject of one of the noblest portraits created by the genius of John Sargent; and that he spent most of his time on board a magnificent yacht, surrounded by a staff of six secretaries.

This was enough, of course, to inspire me with a keen desire to meet Mr. Pulitzer; it was not enough to afford me the slightest idea of what life would be like in close personal contact with such a man.

The general opinion of my friends was that life with Mr. Pulitzer would be one long succession of happy, care-free days spent along the languorous shores of the Mediterranean - days of which perhaps two hours would be devoted to light conversation with my interesting host, and the remainder of my waking moments to the gaities of Monte Carlo, to rambles on the picturesque hillsides of Rapallo and Bordighera, or to the genial companionship of my fellow-secretaries under the snowy awnings of the yacht.

We argued the matter out to our entire satisfaction. Mr. Pulitzer, in addition to being blind, was a chronic invalid, requiring a great deal of sleep and repose. He could hardly be expected to occupy more than twelve hours a day with his secretaries. That worked out at two hours apiece, or, if the division was made by days, about one day a week to each secretary.

The yacht, I had been given to understand, cruised for about eight months in the year over a course bounded by Algiers and the Piraeus, by Mentone and Alexandria, with visits to the ports of Italy, Sicily, Corsica, and Crete. The least imaginative of mortals could make a very fair and alluring picture of what life would be like under such circumstances. As the event turned out it was certainly not our imaginations that were at fault.

As time passed without bringing any further sign from Mr. Tuohy my hopes gradually died out, and I fixed in my mind a date upon which I would abandon all expectations of securing the appointment. Scarcely had I reached this determination when I received a telegram from Mr. Tuohy asking me to lunch with him the next day at the Cafe Royal in order to meet Mr. Ralph Pulitzer, who was passing through London on his way back to America after a visit to his father.

I leave my readers to imagine what sort of a lunch I had in the company of two gentlemen whose duty it was to struggle with the problem of discovering the real character and attainments of a guest who knew he was under inspection.

I found Mr. Ralph Pulitzer to be a slender, clean-cut, pale gentleman of an extremely quiet and self-possessed manner. He was very agreeable, and he listened to my torrent of words with an interest which, if it were real, reflected great credit on me, and which, if it were feigned, reflected not less credit on him.

As we parted he said, "I shall write to my father to-day and tell him of our meeting. Of course, as you know, the decision in this matter rests entirely with him."

After this incident there was another long silence, and I again fixed upon a day beyond which I would not allow my hopes to flourish. The day arrived, nothing happened, and the next morning I went down to the offices of the West India Royal Mail Steam Packet Company and made inquiries about the boats for Barbados. I spent the afternoon at my club making out a list of things to be taken out as aids to comfortable housekeeping in a semi-tropical country - a list which swelled amazingly as I turned over the fascinating pages of the Army and Navy Stores Catalogue.

By dinner time I had become more than reconciled to the new turn of affairs, and when I reached my flat at midnight I found myself impatient of the necessary delay before I could settle down to a life of easy literary activity in one of the most delightful climates in the world and in the neighborhood of a large circle of charming friends and acquaintances.

On the table in the hall I found a telegram from Mr. Tuohy instructing me to start next morning for Mentone, where Mr. Pulitzer would entertain me as his guest for a fortnight, either at his villa or aboard his yacht Liberty, and informing me that I would find at my club early in the morning an envelope containing a ticket to Mentone, with sleeper and parlor-car accommodation, and a check to cover incidental expenses.

The tickets and the check were accompanied by a letter in which I was told that I was to consider this two weeks' visit as a trial, that during that time all my expenses would be paid, that I would receive an honorarium of so much a day from the time I left London until I was engaged by Mr. Pulitzer or had arrived back in London after rejection by him, and that everything depended upon the impression I made on my host.

I left London cold, damp, and foggy; and in less than twenty-four hours I was in the train between Marseilles and Mentone, watching the surf playing among the rocks in the brilliant sunshine of the Cote d'Azur. In the tiny harbor of Mentone I found, anchored stern-on to the quay, the steam yacht Liberty - a miracle of snowy decks and gleaming brass-work - tonnage 1,607, length over all 316 feet, beam 35.6 feet, crew 60, all told.

A message from Mr. Pulitzer awaited me. Would I dine at his villa at Cap Martin? An automobile would call for me at seven o'clock.

I spent the day in looking over the yacht and in trying to pick up some information as to the general lay of the land, by observing every detail of my new surroundings.

The yacht itself claimed my first attention. Everything was new and fascinating to me, for although I had had my share of experiences in barques, and brigs, and full-rigged ships, in mail boats and tramp steamers, only once before had I had an opportunity to examine closely a large private yacht. Ten years before, I had spent some time cruising along the northern coast of Borneo in the yacht of His Highness Sir Charles Brooke, Raja of Sarawak; but with that single exception yachting was for me an unknown phase of sea life.

The Liberty - or, as the secretarial staff, for reasons which will become apparent later, called her, the Liberty, Ha! Ha! - was designed and built on the Clyde. I have never seen a vessel of more beautiful lines. Sailors would find, I think, but one fault in her appearance and one peculiarity. With a white-painted hull, her bridge and the whole of her upper structure, except the masts and funnel, were also white, giving to her general features a certain flatness which masked her fine proportions. Her bridge, instead of being well forward, was placed so far aft that it was only a few feet from the funnel. The object of this departure from custom was to prevent any walking over Mr. Pulitzer's head when he sat in his library, which was situated under the spot, where the bridge would have been in most vessels.

The boat was specially designed to meet Mr. Pulitzer's peculiar requirements. She had a flush deck from the bows to the stern, broken only, for perhaps twenty feet, by a well between the forecastle head and the fore part of the bridge.

Running aft from the bridge to within forty feet of the stern was an unbroken line of deck houses. Immediately afore the bridge was Mr. Pulitzer's library, a handsome room lined from floor to ceiling with books; abaft of that was the dining saloon, which could accommodate in comfort a dozen people;

continuing aft there were, on the port side, the pantry, amidships the enclosed space over the engine room, and on the starboard side a long passage leading to the drawing-room and writing-room used by the secretaries and by members of Mr. Pulitzer's family when they were on the yacht.

The roof and sides of this line of deck houses were extended a few feet beyond the aftermost room, so as to provide a sheltered nook where Mr. Pulitzer could sit when the wind was too strong for his comfort on the open deck.

Between the sides of the deck houses and the sides of the ship there ran on each side a promenade about nine feet broad, unbroken by bolt or nut, stanchion or ventilator, smooth as a billiard table and made of the finest quality of seasoned teak. The promenade continued across the fore part of Mr. Pulitzer's library and across the after part of the line of deck houses, so that there was an oblong track round the greater part of the boat, a track covered overhead with double awnings and protected inboard by the sides of the deck houses, and outboard by adjustable canvas screens, which could be let down or rolled up in a few minutes.

About thirty feet from the stern a heavy double canvas screen ran 'thwartships from one side of the boat to the other, shutting off a small space of deck for the use of the crew. The main deck space was allotted as follows: under the forecastle head accommodation for two officers and two petty officers, abaft of that the well space, of which I have spoken; under the library was Mr. Pulitzer's bedroom, occupying the whole breadth of the ship and extending from the bulkhead at the after part of the well space as far aft as the companion way leading down between the library and the saloon, say twenty-five feet.

A considerable proportion of the sides of this bedroom was given up to books; in one corner was a very high wash-hand-stand, so high that Mr. Pulitzer, who was well over six feet tall, could wash his hands without stooping. The provision of this very high wash-hand-stand illustrates the minute care with which everything had been foreseen in the construction and fitting-up of the yacht. When a person stoops there is a slight impediment to the free flow of blood to the head, such an impediment might react unfavorably on the condition of Mr. Pulitzer's eyes, therefore the wash-hand-stand was high enough to be used without stooping.

In the forward bulkhead of the cabin were two silent fans, one drawing air into the room, the other drawing it out. The most striking feature of the room was an immense four-poster bed which stood in the center of the cabin, with a couch at the foot and one or two chairs at one side. Hanging at the head of the bed was a set of electric push-bells, the cords being of different lengths so that Mr. Pulitzer could call at will for the major-domo, the chief steward, the captain, the officer on watch, and so on.

The bedroom was heavily carpeted and was cut off from the rest of the ship by double bulkheads, double doors, and double portholes, with the object of protecting Mr. Pulitzer as much as possible from all noise, to which he was excessively sensitive. A large bathroom opened immediately off the bedroom, and a flight of steps led down to a gymnasium on the lower deck.

Abaft of Mr. Pulitzer's bedroom there were, on the port side, the cabins of the major-domo, the captain, the head butler, the chief engineer, an officers' mess room, the ship's galley, a steward's mess room, and the cabins of the chief steward and one or two officers.

Corresponding with these there were, on the starboard side, the cabins of the secretaries and the doctor, "The Cells," as we called them. They were comfortable rooms, all very much on one pattern, except that of the business secretary, which was a good deal larger than the others. He needed the additional space for newspaper files, documents, correspondence, and so on. Each cabin contained a bed, a wash-hand-stand, a chest of drawers, a cupboard for clothes, a small folding table, some book shelves, an arm chair, an ordinary chair, an electric fan, and a radiator. Each cabin had two portholes, and there were two bathrooms to the six cabins.

The center of the ship, between these cabins and the corresponding space on the port side, was occupied by the engine room; and the entrance to the secretaries' quarters was through a companionway opening on to the promenade deck, with a door on each side of the yacht, and leading down a flight of stairs to a long fore-and-aft passage, out of which all the secretaries' cabins opened.

Abaft the secretaries' cabins, and occupying the whole breadth of the boat, were a number of cabins and suites for the accommodation of Mrs. Pulitzer, other members of the family, and guests; and abaft of these, cut off by a 'thwartships bulkhead, were the quarters of the crew.

The lower deck was given over chiefly to stores, coal bunkers, the engine room, the stoke-hold, and to a large number of electric accumulators, which kept the electric lights going when the engines were not working. There were, however, on this deck the gymnasium, and a large room, directly under Mr. Pulitzer's bedroom, used to take the overflow from the library.

The engines were designed rather for smooth running than for speed, and twelve knots an hour was the utmost that could be got out of them, the average running speed being about eight knots. The yacht had an ample supply of boats, including two steam launches, one burning coal, the other oil.

During my inspection of the yacht I was accompanied by my cabin-steward, a young Englishman who had at one time served aboard the German Emperor's yacht, Meteor. Nothing could have been more courteous than his manner or more intelligent than his explanations; but the moment I tried to draw him out on the subject of life on the yacht he relapsed into a vagueness from which I could extract no gleam of enlightenment. After fencing for some time with my queries he suggested that I might like to have a glass of sherry and a biscuit in the secretaries' library, and, piloting me thither, he left me.

The smoking-room was furnished with writing tables, some luxurious arm chairs, and a comfortable lounge, and every spare nook was filled with book shelves. The contents of these shelves were extremely varied. A cursory glance showed me Meyer's Neues Konversations-Lexicon, The Yacht Register, Whitaker's Almanack, Who's Who, Burke's Peerage, The Almanack de Gotha, the British and the Continental Bradshaw, a number of Baedeker's "Guides," fifty or sixty volumes of the Tauchnitz edition, a large collection of files of reviews and magazines - The Nineteenth Century, Quarterly, Edinburgh, Fortnightly, Contemporary, National, Atlantic, North American, Revue de Deux Mondes - and a scattering of volumes by Kipling, Shaw, Hosebery, Pater, Ida Tarbell, Bryce, Ferrero, Macaulay, Anatole France, Maupassant, "Dooley," and a large number of French and German plays. I was struck by the entire absence of books of travel and scientific works.

I spent part of the afternoon in the drawing-room playing a large instrument of the gramophone type. There were several hundred records - from grand opera, violin solos by Kreisler, and the Gilbert and Sullivan operas, to rag-time and the latest comic songs.

Before the time came to dress for dinner I had met the captain and some of the officers of the yacht. They were all very civil; and my own experience as a sailor enabled me to see that they were highly efficient men. I was a good deal puzzled, however, by something peculiar but very elusive in their attitude toward me, something which I had at once detected in the manner of my cabin-steward.

With their courtesy was mingled a certain flavor of curiosity tinged with amusement, which, so far from being offensive, was distinctly friendly, but which, nevertheless, gave me a vague sense of uneasiness. In fact the whole atmosphere of the yacht was one of restlessness and suspense; and the effect was heightened because each person who spoke to me appeared to be on the point of divulging some secret or delivering some advice, which discretion checked at his lips.

I felt myself very much under observation, a feeling as though I was a new boy in a boarding school or a new animal at the zoo - interesting to my companions not only on account of my novelty, but because my personal peculiarities would affect the comfort of the community of which I was to become a member.

At seven o'clock my cabin-steward announced the arrival of the automobile, and after a swift run along the plage and up the winding roads on the hillsides of Cap Martin I found myself at the door of Mr. Pulitzer's villa. I was received by the major-domo, ushered into the drawing-room, and informed that Mr. Pulitzer would be down in a few minutes.

CHAPTER II

MEETING JOSEPH PULITZER

Before I had time to examine my surroundings Mr. Pulitzer entered the room on the arm of the major-domo. My first swift impression was of a very tall man with broad shoulders, the rest of the body tapering away to thinness, with a noble head, bushy reddish beard streaked with gray, black hair, swept back from the forehead and lightly touched here and there with silvery white. One eye was dull and half closed, the other was of a deep, brilliant blue which, so far from suggesting blindness, created the instant effect of a searching, eagle-like glance. The outstretched hand was large, strong, nervous, full of character, ending in well-shaped and immaculately kept nails.

A high-pitched voice, clear, penetrating, and vibrant, gave out the strange challenge: "Well, here you see before you the miserable wreck who is to be your host; you must make the best you can of him. Give me your arm into dinner."

I may complete here a description of Mr. Pulitzer's appearance, founded upon months of close personal association with him. The head was splendidly modeled, the forehead high, the brows prominent and arched; the ears were large, the nose was long and hooked; the mouth, almost concealed by the mustache, was firm and thin-lipped; the jaws showed square and powerful under the beard; the length of the face was much emphasized by the flowing beard and by the way in which the hair was brushed back from the forehead. The skin was of a clear, healthy pink, like a young girl's; but in moments of intense excitement the color would deepen to a dark, ruddy flush, and after a succession of sleepless nights, or under the strain of continued worry, it would turn a dull, lifeless gray.

I have never seen a face which varied so much in expression. Not only was there a marked difference at all times between one side and the other, due partly to the contrast between the two eyes and partly to a loss of flexibility in the muscles of the right side, but almost from moment to moment the general appearance of the face moved between a lively, genial animation, a cruel and wolf-like scowl, and a heavy and hopeless dejection. No face was capable of showing greater tenderness; none could assume a more forbidding expression of anger and contempt.

The Sargent portrait, a masterpiece of vivid character-painting, is a remarkable revelation of the complex nature of its subject. It discloses the deep affection, the keen intelligence, the wide sympathy, the tireless energy, the delicate sensitiveness, the tearing impatience, the cold tyranny, and the flaming scorn by which his character was so erratically dominated. It is a noble and pathetic monument to the suffering which had been imposed for a quarter of a century upon the intense and arbitrary spirit of this extraordinary man.

The account which I am to give of Mr. Pulitzer's daily life during the months immediately preceding his death would be unintelligible to all but the very few who knew him in recent years if it were not prefaced by a brief biographical note.

Joseph Pulitzer was born in the village of Mako, near Buda Pesth in Hungary, on April 10, 1847. His father was a Jew, his mother a Christian. At the age of sixteen he emigrated to the United States. He landed without friends, without money, unable to speak a word of English. He enlisted immediately in the First New York (Lincoln) Cavalry Regiment, a regiment chiefly composed of Germans and in which German was the prevailing tongue.

Within a year the Civil War ended, and Pulitzer found himself, in common with hundreds of thousands of others, out of employment at a time when employment was most difficult to secure. At this time he was so poor that he was turned away from French's Hotel for lack of fifty cents with which to pay for his bed. In less than twenty years he bought French's Hotel, pulled it down, and erected in its place the Pulitzer Building, at that time one of the largest business buildings in New York, where he housed The World.

What lay between these two events may be summed up in a few words. At the close of the Civil War Mr. Pulitzer went to St. Louis, and in 1868, after being engaged in various occupations, he became a reporter on the Westliche Post. In less than ten years he was editor and part proprietor. His amazing energy, his passionate interest in politics, his rare gift of terse and forcible expression, and his striking personality carried him over or through all obstacles.

After he had purchased the St. Louis Dispatch, amalgamated it with the Post, and made the Post-Dispatch a profitable business enterprise and a power to be reckoned with in politics, he felt the need of a wider field in which to maneuver the forces of his character and his intellect.

He came to New York in 1883 and purchased The World from Jay Gould. At that time The World had a circulation of less than twelve thousand copies a day, and was practically bankrupt. From this time forward Mr. Pulitzer concentrated his every faculty on building up The World. He was scoffed at, ridiculed, and abused by the most powerful editors of the old school. They were to learn, not without bitterness and wounds, that opposition was the one fuel of all others which best fed the triple flame of his courage, his tenacity, and his resourcefulness.

Four years of unremitting toil produced two results. The

World reached a circulation of two hundred thousand copies a day and took its place in the front rank of the American press as a journal of force and ability, and Joseph Pulitzer left New York, a complete nervous wreck, to face in solitude the knowledge that he would never read print again and that within a few years he would be totally blind.

Joseph Pulitzer, as I knew him twenty-four years after he had been driven from active life by the sudden and final collapse of his health, was a man who could be judged by no common standards, for his feelings, his temper, and his point of view had been warped by years of suffering.

Had his spirit been broken by his trials, had his intellectual power weakened under the load of his affliction, had his burning interest in affairs cooled to a point where he could have been content to turn his back upon life's conflict, he might have found some happiness, or at least some measure of repose akin to that with which age consoles us for the loss of youth. But his greatest misfortune was that all the active forces of his personality survived to the last in their full vigor, inflicting upon him the curse of an impatience which nothing could appease, of a discontent which knew no amelioration.

My first meeting with Mr. Pulitzer is indelibly fixed in my memory. As we entered the dining-room the butler motioned to me to take a seat on Mr. Pulitzer's right hand, and as I did so I glanced up and down the table to find myself in the presence of half-a-dozen gentlemen in evening dress, who bowed in a very friendly manner as Mr. Pulitzer said, with a broad sweep of his hand, "Gentlemen, this is Mr. Alleyne Ireland; you will be able to inform him later of my fads and crotchets; well, don't be ungenerous with me, don't paint the devil as black as he is."

This was spoken in a tone of banter, and was cut short by a curious, prolonged chuckle, which differed from laughter in the feeling it produced in the hearer that the mirth did not spring from the open, obvious humor of the situation, but from some whimsical thought which was the more relished because its nature was concealed from us. I felt that, instead of my host's amusement having been produced by his peculiar introduction, he had made his eccentric address merely as an excuse to chuckle over some notion which had formed itself in his mind from material entirely foreign to his immediate surroundings.

I mention this because I found later that one of Mr. Pulitzer's most embarrassing peculiarities was the sudden revelation from time to time of a mental state entirely at odds with the occupation of the moment. In the middle of an account of a play, when I was doing my best to reproduce some scene from memory, with appropriate changes of voice to represent the different characters, Mr. Pulitzer would suddenly break in, "Did we ever get a reply to that letter about Laurier's speech on reciprocity? No? Well, all right, go on, go on."

Or it might be when I was reading from the daily papers an account of a murder or a railroad wreck that Mr. Pulitzer would break out into a peal of his peculiar chuckling laughter. I would immediately stop reading, when he would pat me on the arm, and say, "Go on, boy, go on, don't mind me. I wasn't laughing at you. I was thinking of something else. What was it? Oh, a railroad wreck, well, don't stop, go on reading."

As soon as we were seated Mr. Pulitzer turned to me and began to question me about my reading. Had I read any recent fiction? No? Well, what had I read within the past month?

I named several books which I had been re-reading - Macaulay's Essays, Meredith Townsend's Asia and Europe, and Lowes Dickinson's Modern Symposium.

"Well, tell me something about Asia and Europe" he said.

I left my dinner untasted, and for a quarter of an hour held forth on the life of Mohammed, on the courage of the Arabians, on the charm of Asia for Asiatics, and on other matters taken from Mr. Townsend's fascinating book. Suddenly Mr. Pulitzer interrupted me.

"My God! You don't mean to tell me that anyone is interested in that sort of rubbish. Everybody knows about Mohammed, and about the bravery of the Arabs, and, for God's sake, why shouldn't Asia be attractive to the Asiatics! Try something else. Do you remember any plays?"

Yes, I remembered several pretty well. Shaw's Caesar and Cleopatra for instance.

"Go on, then, try and tell me about that."

My prospects of getting any dinner faded away as I began my new effort. Fortunately I knew the play very well, and remembered a number of passages almost word for word. I soon saw that Mr. Pulitzer was interested and pleased, not with the play as anything new to him, for he probably knew it better than I did, but with my presentation of it, because it showed some ability to compress narrative without destroying its character and also gave some proof of a good memory.

When I reached the scene in which Caesar replies to Britannus's protest against the recognition of Cleopatra's marriage to her brother, Ptolemy, by saying, "Pardon him, Theodotus; he is a barbarian, and thinks that the customs of his tribe are the laws of nature," Mr. Pulitzer burst into an uncontrollable fit of laughter.

I was about to continue, and try to make good better, when Mr. Pulitzer raised his hands above his head in remonstrance.

"Stop! Stop! For God's sake! You're hurting me," very much as a person with a cracked lip begs for mercy when you are in the middle of your most humorous story.

I found out later that, in order to keep in Mr. Pulitzer's good graces, it was as necessary to avoid being too funny as it was to avoid being too dull, for, while the latter fault hurt his intellectual sensitiveness, the former involved, through the excessive laughter it produced, a degree of involuntary exertion which, in his disordered physical condition, caused him acute pain.

Mr. Pulitzer's constant use of the exclamations "My God!" and "For God's sake!" had no relation whatever to swearing, as the term is usually understood; they were employed exactly as a French lady employs the exclamation Mon Dieu! or a German the expression Ach, du liebe Gott! As a matter of fact, although Mr. Pulitzer was a man of strong and, at times, violent emotions, and, from his deplorable nervous state, excessively irritable, I do not think that in the eight months I was with him, during the greater part of which time he was not under any restraining influence, such as might be exerted by the presence of ladies, I heard him use any oath except occasionally a "damn," which appealed to him, I think, as a suitable if not a necessary qualification of the word "fool." For Mr. Pulitzer there were no fools except damned fools.

After the excitement about Caesar and Cleopatra had subsided, Mr. Pulitzer asked me if I had a good memory. I hesitated before replying, because I had seen enough of Mr. Pulitzer in an hour to realize that a constant exercise of caution would be necessary if I wished to avoid offending his prejudices or wounding his susceptibilities; and whereas on the one hand I did not wish to set a standard for myself which I would find it impossible to live up to, on the other hand I was anxious to avoid giving any description of my abilities which would be followed later by a polite intimation from the major-domo that Mr. Pulitzer had enjoyed my visit immensely but that I was not just the man for the place.

So I compromised and said that I had a fairly good memory.

"Well, everybody thinks he's got a good memory," replied Mr. Pulitzer.

"I only claimed a fairly good one," I protested.

"Oh! that's just an affectation; as a matter of fact you think you've got a splendid memory, don't you? Now, be frank about it; I love people to be frank with me."

My valor got the better of my discretion, and I replied that if he really wished me to be frank I was willing to admit that I had no particular desire to lay claim to a good memory, for I was inclined to accept the view which I had once heard expressed by a very wise man of my acquaintance that the human mind was not intended to remember with but to think with, and that one of the greatest benefits which had been conferred on mankind by the discovery of printing was that thousands of things could be recorded for reference which former generations had been compelled to learn by rote.

"Your wise friend," he cried, "was a damned fool! If you will give the matter a moment's thought you'll see that memory is the highest faculty of the human mind. What becomes of all your reading, all your observation, your experience, study, investigations, discussions - in a rushing crescendo - if you have no memory?"

"I might reply," I said, "by asking what use it is to lumber up your mind with a mass of information of which you are only going to make an occasional use when you can have it filed away in encyclopedias and other works of reference, and in card indexes, instantly available when you want it."

I spoke in a light and rather humorous tone in order to take the edge off my dissent from his opinion, reflecting that even between friends and equals a demand for frankness is most safely to be regarded as a danger signal to impulsiveness; but it was too late, I had evidently overstepped the mark, for Mr. Pulitzer turned abruptly from me without replying, and began to talk to the gentleman on his left.

This had the twofold advantage of giving me time to

Alleyne Ireland

reconsider my strategy, and to eat some dinner, which one of the footmen, evidently the kind with a memory for former experiences, had set on one side and kept warm against the moment when I would be free to enjoy it.

As I ate I listened to the conversation. It made my heart sink. The gentleman to whom Mr. Pulitzer had transferred his attentions was a Scotchman, Mr. William Romaine Paterson. I discovered later that he was the nearest possible approach to a walking encyclopedia. His range of information was - well, I am tempted to say, infamous. He appeared to have an exhaustive knowledge of French, German, Italian, and English literature, of European history in its most complicated ramifications, and of general biography in such a measure that, in regard to people as well known as Goethe, Voltaire, Kossuth, Napoleon, Garibaldi, Bismarck, and a score of others, he could fix a precise day on which any event or conversation had taken place, and recall it in its minutest details.

It was not simply from the standpoint of my own ignorance that Paterson's store of knowledge assumed such vast proportions, for it was seldom opened except in the presence of Mr. Pulitzer, in whom were combined a tenacious memory, a profound acquaintance with the subjects which Paterson had taken for his province, an analytic mind, and a zest for contradiction. Everything Paterson said was immediately pounced upon by a vigorous, astute, and well-informed critic who derived peculiar satisfaction from the rare instances in which he could detect him in an inaccuracy.

The conversation between Mr. Pulitzer and Paterson, or, rather, Paterson's frequently interrupted monologue, lasted until we had all finished dinner, and the butler had lighted Mr. Pulitzer's cigar. In the middle of an eloquent passage from Paterson, Mr. Pulitzer rose, turned abruptly toward me, held out his hand, and said, "I'm very glad to have met you, Mr. Ireland; you have entertained me very much. Please come here to-morrow at eleven o'clock, and I'll take you out for a drive. Good-night." He took Paterson's arm and left the room.

The door, like all the doors in Mr. Pulitzer's various residences, shut automatically and silently; and after one of the secretaries had drawn a heavy velvet curtain across the doorway, so that not the faintest sound could escape from the room, I was chaffed good-naturedly about my debut as a candidate. To my great surprise I was congratulated on having done very well.

"You made a great hit," said one, "with your account of Shaw's play."

"I nearly burst out laughing," said another, "when you gave your views about memory. I think you're dead right about it; but J. P. - Mr. Pulitzer was always referred to as J. P. - is crazy about people having good memories, so if you've really got a good memory you'd better let him find it out."

I was told that, so far as we were concerned, the day's work, or at least that portion of it which involved being with J. P., was to be considered over as soon as he retired to the library after dinner. His object then was to be left alone with one secretary, who read to him until about ten o'clock, when the major-domo came and took him to his rooms for the night. As a rule, J. P. made no further demand on the bodily presence of his secretaries after he had gone to bed, but occasionally, when he could not sleep, one of them would be called, perhaps at three in the morning, to read to him.

This meant in practice that, when we were ashore, one, or more usually two of us, would remain in the house in case of emergency. This did not by any means imply that we were always free from work after ten o'clock at night, in fact the very opposite was true, for it was J. P.'s custom to say, during dinner, that on the following day he would ride, drive, or walk with such a one or such a one, naming him; and the victim - a term frequently used with a good deal of surprisingly frank enjoyment by J. P. himself - had often to work well into the night preparing material for conversation.

I saw something of what this preparation meant before I left the villa after my first meeting with J. P. Two of the secretaries said they would go over to Monte Carlo, and they asked me to go with them; but I declined, preferring to remain behind for a chat with one of the secretaries, Mr. Norman G. Thwaites, an Englishman, who was secretary in a more technical sense than any of the rest of us, for he was a shorthand writer and did most of J. P.'s correspondence.

After the others had gone he showed me a table in the entrance hall of the villa, on which was a big pile of mail just arrived from London. It included a great number of newspapers and weeklies, several copies of each. There were The Times, The Daily Telegraph, The Daily Mail, The Morning Post, The Daily News, The Westminster Gazette, Truth, The Spectator, The Saturday Review, The Nation, The Outlook, and some other London publications, as well as the Paris editions of the New York Herald and The Daily Mail.

Thwaites selected a copy of each and then led the way to his bedroom, a large room on the top floor, from which we could see across the bay the brilliant lights of Monte Carlo.

He then explained to me that he had been selected to read to J. P. whilst the latter had his breakfast and his after-breakfast cigar the next morning. In order to do this satisfactorily he had to go over the papers and read carefully whatever he could find that was suited to J. P.'s taste at that particular time of the day. During the breakfast hour J. P. would not have anything read to him which was of an exciting nature. This preference excluded political news, crime, disaster, and war correspondence, and left practically nothing but book reviews, criticisms of plays, operas, and art exhibitions, and publishers' announcements.

The principal sources of information on these topics were the literary supplement of the London Times, the Literary Digest, and the literary, dramatic, and musical columns of the Athenaeum, The Spectator, and the Saturday Review.

These had to be "prepared," to use J. P.'s phrase, which meant that they were read over rapidly once and then gone over again with some concentration so that the more important articles could be marked for actual reading, the other portions being dealt with conversationally, everything being boiled down to its essence before it reached Mr. Pulitzer's ear.

As it was getting late, and as I knew that Thwaites would be on tap early in the morning, for J. P. usually breakfasted before nine, and the "victim" was supposed to have had his own breakfast by eight, I left the villa and went back to the yacht.

As he said good-night, Thwaites gave me a copy of The Daily Telegraph and advised me to read it carefully, as J. P. might ask me for the day's news during the drive we were to take the following morning.

Before going to sleep I glanced through The Daily Telegraph and came across an article which gave me an idea for establishing my reputation for memory. It was a note about the death duties which had been collected in England during 1910, and it gave a list of about twenty estates on which large sums had been paid. The list included the names of the deceased and also the amounts on which probate duty had been paid. I decided to commit these names and figures to memory and to take an occasion the next day to reel them off to J. P.

Punctually at eleven o'clock I presented myself at the villa to find, to my dismay, J. P. seated in his automobile in a towering rage. What sort of consideration had I for him to keep him waiting for half an hour!

I protested that eleven o'clock was the hour of the appointment. I was absolutely wrong, he said, half-past-ten was the time, and he remembered perfectly naming that hour, because he wanted a long drive and he had an engagement with Mr. Paterson at noon.

"I'm awfully sorry," I began, "if I misunderstood you, but really..."

He dismissed the matter abruptly by saying, "For God's sake, don't argue about it. Get in and sit next to me so that I can hear you talk."

As soon as we had got clear of the village, and were spinning along at a good rate on the Corniche road, which circles the Bay of Monaco, high on the mountain side, Mr. Pulitzer began to put me through my paces.

"Now, Mr. Ireland," he began, "you will understand that if any arrangement is to be concluded between us I must explore your brain, your character, your tastes, your sympathies, your prejudices, your temper; I must find out if you have tact, patience, a sense of humor, the gift of condensing information, and, above all, a respect, a love, a passion for accuracy."

I began to speak, but he interrupted me before I had got six words out of my mouth.

"Wait! Wait!" he cried, "let me finish what I have to say. You'll find this business of being a candidate a very trying and disagreeable one; well, it's damned disagreeable to me, too. What I need is rest, repose, quiet, routine, understanding, sympathy, friendship, yes, my God! the friendship of those around me. Mr. Ireland, I can do much, I can do everything for a man who will be my friend. I can give him power, I can give him wealth, I can give him reputation, the power, the wealth, the reputation which come to a man who speaks to a million people a day in the columns of a great paper. But how am I to do this? I am blind, I'm an invalid; how am I to know whom I can trust? I don't mean in money matters; money's nothing to me; it can do nothing for me; I mean morally, intellectually. I've had scores of people pass through my hands in the last fifteen years - Englishmen, Scotchmen, Irishmen, Welshmen, Germans, Frenchmen, Americans, men of so-called high family, men of humble birth, men from a dozen universities, self-taught men, young men, old men, and, my God! what have I found? Arrogance, stupidity, ingratitude, loose thinking, conceit, ignorance, laziness, indifference; absence of tact, discretion, courtesy, manners, consideration, sympathy, devotion; no knowledge, no wisdom, no intelligence, no observation, no memory, no insight, no understanding. My God! I can hardly believe my own experience when I think of it."

Set down in cold print, this outburst loses almost every trace of its intensely dramatic character. Mr. Pulitzer spoke as though he were declaiming a part in a highly emotional play. At times he turned toward me, his clenched fists raised above his shoulders, at times he threw back his head, flung his outstretched hands at arms' length in front of him, as though he were appealing to the earth, to the sea, to the air, to the remote canopy of the sky to hear his denunciation of man's inefficiency; at times he paused, laid a hand on my arm, and fixed his eye upon me as if he expected the darkness to yield him some image of my thought. It was almost impossible to believe at such a moment that he was totally blind, that he could not distinguish night from day.

"Mind!" he continued, raising a cautionary finger, "I'm not making any criticism of my present staff; you may consider yourself very lucky if I find you to have a quarter of the good qualities which any one of them has; and let me tell you that while you are with me you will do well to observe these gentlemen and to try and model yourself on them.

"However, all that doesn't matter so much in your case, because there's no question of your becoming one of my personal staff. I haven't any vacancy at present, and I don't foresee any. What I want you for is something quite different."

Imagine my amazement. No vacancy on the staff! What about the advertisement I had answered? What about all the interviews and correspondence, in which a companionship had been the only thing discussed? What could the totally different thing be of which Mr. Pulitzer spoke?

In the midst of my confusion Mr. Pulitzer said, "Look out of the window and tell me what you see. Remember that I am blind, and try and make me get a mental picture of everything - everything, you understand; never think that anything is too small or insignificant to be of interest to me; you can't tell what may interest me; always describe everything with the greatest minuteness, every cloud in the sky, every shadow on the hillside, every tree, every house, every dress, every wrinkle on a face, everything, everything!"

I did my best, and he appeared to be pleased; but before I had half exhausted the details of the magnificent scene above and below us he stopped me suddenly with a request that I should tell him exactly what had occurred from the time I had answered his advertisement up to the moment of my arrival at the villa.

This demand placed me in rather an awkward predicament, for I had to try and reconcile the fact that the advertisement itself as well as all my conversations with his agents and with his son had been directed toward the idea of a companionship, with his positive assertion that there was no vacancy on his personal staff and that he wanted me for another, and an undisclosed purpose. Here was a very clear opportunity for destroying my reputation, either for tact or for accuracy.

There was, of course, only one thing to do, and that was to tell him exactly what had taken place. This I did, and at the end of my recital he said, "It's simply amazing how anyone can get a matter tangled up the way you have. There was never a question of your becoming one of my companions. What I want is a man to go out to the Philippines and write a series of vigorous articles showing the bungle we've made of that business, and paving the way for an agitation in favor of giving the Islands their independence. There'll be a chance of getting that done if we elect a Democratic President in 1912."

"Well, sir," I replied, "if the bungle has been as bad as you think I certainly ought to be able to do the work to your satisfaction. I'm pretty familiar with the conditions of tropical life, I've written a good deal on the subject, I've been in the Philippines and have published a book and a number of articles about them, and, although I don't take as gloomy a view as you do about the administration out there, I found a good deal to criticize, and if I go out I can certainly describe the conditions as they are now, and your editorial writers can put my articles to whatever use they may wish."

"You're going too fast," he said, "and you're altogether too cock-sure of your abilities. You mustn't think that because you've written articles for the London Times you are competent to write for The World. It's a very different matter. The American people want something terse, forcible, picturesque, striking, something that will arrest their attention, enlist their sympathy, arouse their indignation, stimulate their imagination, convince their reason, awaken their conscience. Why should I accept you at your own estimate? You don't realize the responsibility I have in this matter. The World isn't like your Times, with its forty or fifty thousand educated readers. It's read by, well, say a million people a day; and it's my duty to see that they get the truth; but that's not enough, I've got to put it before them briefly so that they will read it, clearly so that they will understand it, forcibly so that they will appreciate it, picturesquely so that they will remember it, and, above all, accurately so that they may be wisely guided by its light. And you come to me, and before you've been here a day you ask me to entrust you with an important mission which concerns the integrity of my paper, the conscience of my readers, the policy of my country, no, my God! you're too cock-sure of yourself."

By this time Mr. Pulitzer had worked himself up into a state of painful excitement. His forehead was damp with perspiration, he clasped and unclasped his hands, his voice became louder and higher-pitched from moment to moment; but when he suddenly stopped speaking he calmed down instantly.

"You shouldn't let me talk so much," he said, without, however, suggesting any means by which I could stop him. "What time is it? Are we nearly home? Well, Mr. Ireland, I'll let you off for the afternoon; go and enjoy yourself and forget all about me." Then, as the auto drew up at the door of the villa, "Come up to dinner about seven and try to be amusing. You did very well last night. I hope you can keep it up. It's most important that anyone who is to live with me should have a sense of humor. I'd be glad to keep a man and pay him a handsome salary if he would make me laugh once a day. Well, good-by till to-night."

CHAPTER III

LIFE AT CAP MARTIN

There was no lack of humor in Mr. Pulitzer's suggestion that I should go and enjoy myself and forget him. I went down to the yacht, had lunch in solitary state, and then, selecting a comfortable chair in the smoking-room, settled down to think things over.

It soon became clear to me that J. P. was a man of a character so completely outside the range of my experience that any skill of judgment I might have acquired through contact with many men of many races would avail me little in my intercourse with him.

That he was arbitrary, self-centered, and exacting mattered little to me; it was a combination of qualities which rumor had led me to expect in him, and with which I had become familiar in my acquaintance with men of wide authority and outstanding ability. What disturbed me was that his blindness, his ill health, and his suffering had united to these traits an intense excitability and a morbid nervousness.

My first impulse was to attribute his capriciousness to a weakening of his brain power; but I could not reconcile this view with the vigor of his thought, with the clearness of his expression, with the amplitude of his knowledge, with the scope of his memory as they had been disclosed the previous night in his conversation with Paterson. No, the fact was that I had not found the key to his motives, the cipher running through the artificial confusion of his actions.

I could not foresee the issue of the adventure. In the meantime, however, the yacht was a comfortable home, the Cote d'Azur was a new field of observation, J. P. and his secretaries were extremely interesting, the honorarium was accumulating steadily, and in the background Barbados still slept in the sunshine, an emerald in a sapphire sea.

During the afternoon I had a visit from Jabez E. Dunningham, the major-domo. I pay tribute to him here as one of the most remarkable men I have ever met, an opinion which I formed after months of daily intercourse with him. He was an Englishman, and he had spent nearly twenty years with Mr. Pulitzer, traveling with him everywhere, hardly ever separated from him for more than a few hours, and he was more closely in his confidence than anyone outside the family.

He was capable and efficient in the highest degree. His duties ranged from those of a nurse to those of a diplomat. He produced, at a moment's notice, as a conjuror produces rabbits and goldfish, the latest hot-water bottle from a village pharmacy in Elba, special trains from haughty and reluctant officials of State railways, bales of newspapers mysteriously collected from clubs, hotels, or consulates in remote and microscopic ports, fruits and vegetables out of season, rooms, suites, floors of hotels at the height of the rush in the most crowded resorts, or a dozen cabins in a steamer.

He could open telegraph stations and post offices when they were closed to the native nobility, convert the eager curiosity of port officials into a trance-like indifference, or monopolize the services of a whole administration, if the comfort, convenience, or caprice of his master demanded it.

More than this; if, any of these things having been done, they should appear undesirable to Mr. Pulitzer, Dunningham could undo them with the same magician-like ease as had marked their achievement. A wave of Mr. Pulitzer's hand was translated into action by Dunningham, and the whole of his arrangements disappeared as completely as if they had never existed. The slate was wiped clean, ready in an instant to receive the new message from Mr. Pulitzer's will.

Dunningham had come to offer me advice. I must not be disturbed by the apparent eccentricity of Mr. Pulitzer's conduct; it was merely part of Mr. Pulitzer's fixed policy to make things as complicated and difficult as possible for a candidate. By adopting this plan he was able to discover very quickly whether there was any possibility that a new man would suit him. If the candidate showed impatience or bad temper he could be got rid of at once; if he showed tact and good humor he would graduate into another series of tests, and so on, step by step, until the period of his trying out was ended and he became one of the staff.

A man of my intelligence would, of course, appreciate the advantages of such a method, even from the standpoint of the candidate, for once a candidate had passed the testing stage he would find his relations with Mr. Pulitzer much pleasanter and his work less exacting, whereas if he found at the outset that the conditions were not pleasing to him he could retire without having wasted much time.

One thing I must bear in mind, namely, that each day which passed without Mr. Pulitzer having decided against a candidate increased the candidate's chances. If a man was to be rejected it was usually done inside of a week from his first appearance on the scene.

And, by the way, had I ever noticed how people were apt to think that blind people were deaf? A most curious thing; really nothing in it. Take Mr. Pulitzer, for example, so far from his being deaf he had the most exquisite sense of hearing, in fact he heard better when people spoke below rather than above their ordinary tone.

Thus, Dunningham, anxious, in his master's interest, to allay my nervousness, which reacted disagreeably on Mr. Pulitzer, and to make me lower my voice.

I went up to the villa during the afternoon to look at the house and, if possible, to have a talk with some of the secretaries.

The villa lay on the Western slope of Cap Martin, a few hundred yards from the Villa Cyrnos, occupied by the Empress Eugenie. Seen from the road there was nothing striking in its appearance, but seen from the other side it was delightful, recalling the drop scene of a theater. Situated on a steep slope, embowered in trees, its broad stone veranda overhung a series of ornamental terraces decorated with palms, flowers, statuary, and fountains; and where these ended a jumble of rocks and stunted pines fell away abruptly to the blue water of the bay.

The house was large and well designed, but very simple in its furniture and decorations. The upper rooms on the Western side commanded a superb view of the Bay of Monaco, and of the rugged hillsides above La Turbie, crowned with a vague outline of fortifications against the sky.

In a room at the top of the house I found one of the secretaries, an Englishman, Mr. George Craven, formerly in the Indian Civil Service in Rajputana. He was engaged in auditing the accounts of the yacht, but he readily fell in with my suggestion that we should take a stroll.

"Right-ho!" he said. "I'm sick of these beastly accounts. But we must find out what J. P.'s doing first."

It appeared that J. P. had motored over to Monte Carlo to hear a concert, and that he wasn't expected back for an hour or more. As we stopped in the entrance hall to get our hats I struck a match on the sole of my shoe, intending to light a cigarette.

"By Jove! Don't do that, for Heaven's sake," said Craven, "or there'll be a frightful row when J. P. comes in. He can't stand cigarette smoke, and he's got a sense of smell as keen as a setter's."

We went into the garden and followed a narrow path which led down to the waterside. We talked about J. P. As a matter of fact, J. P. was the principal topic of conversation whenever two of his secretaries found themselves together.

Craven, however, had only been with J. P. for a few weeks, having been one of the batch sifted out of the six hundred who had answered the Times advertisement. He was almost as much in the dark as I was in regard to the real J. P. that existed somewhere behind the mask which was always held out in front of every emotion, every thought, every intention.

The life was difficult, he found, and extremely laborious. When it suited his book J. P. could be one of the most fascinating and entertaining of men, but when it didn't, well, he wasn't. The truth was that you could never tell what he really thought at any moment; it made you feel as though you were blind and not he; you found yourself groping around all the time for a good lead and coming unexpectedly up against a stone wall.

"I've been with him a couple of months," he said, "and I haven't the slightest idea whether he thinks me a good sort or a silly ass, and I don't suppose I ever shall know. By Jove, there he is now!" as we heard the crunch of tires on the drive. "Excuse me if I make a run for it; he may want me any minute. See you later."

At dinner that night Mr. Pulitzer devoted his whole attention to laying bare the vast areas of ignorance on the map of my information. He carried me from country to country, from century to century, through history, art, literature, biography, economics, music, the drama, and current politics. Whenever he hit upon some small spot where my investigations had

Alleyne Ireland

lingered and where my memory served me he left it immediately, with the remark, "Well, I don't care about that; that doesn't amount to anything, anyhow."

It was worse than useless to make any pretense of knowing things, for if you said you knew a play, for instance, J. P. would say, "Good! Now begin at the second scene of the third act, where the curtain rises on the two conspirators in the courtyard of the hotel; just carry it along from there" - and if you didn't know it thoroughly you were soon in difficulties.

His method was nicely adjusted to his needs, for he was concerned most of the time to get entertainment as well as information; and he was, therefore, amused by exposing your ignorance when he was not informed by uncovering your knowledge. Indeed, nothing put him in such good humor as to discover a cleft in your intellectual armor, provided that you really possessed some talent, faculty, or resource which was useful to him.

My dinner, considered as a dinner, was as great a failure as my conversation, considered as an exhibition of learning. I got no more than a hasty mouthful now and again, and got that only through a device often resorted to by the secretaries under such circumstances, but which seldom met with much success.

J. P. himself had to eat, and from time to time the butler, who always stood behind J. P.'s chair, and attended to him only, would take advantage of an instant's pause in the conversation to say, "Your fish is getting cold, sir."

This would divert J. P.'s attention from his victim long enough to allow one of the other men to break in with a remark designed to draw J. P.'s fire. It worked once in a while, but as a rule it had no effect whatever beyond making J. P. hurry through the course so that he could renew his attack at the point where he had suspended it.

On the particular occasion I am describing I was fortunate

enough toward the end of dinner to regain some of the ground I had lost in my disorderly flight across the field of scholarship. One of the secretaries seized an opportunity to refer to the British death duties. I had intended to arrange for the introduction of this topic, but had forgotten to do so. It was just sheer good luck, and I made signs to the gentleman to keep it up. He did so, and the moment he ceased speaking I took up the tale. It was a good subject, for J. P. was interested in the question of death duties.

After a preliminary flourish I began to reel off the figures I had committed to memory the previous night. Before I had got very far Mr. Pulitzer cried.

"Stop! Are you reading those figures?"

"No," I replied. "I read them over last night in the Daily Telegraph."

"My God! Are you giving them from memory? Haven't you got a note of them in your hand? Hasn't he? Hasn't he? ..." appealing to the table.

Reassured on this point he said, "Well, go on, go on. This interests me."

As soon as I had finished he turned to Craven and said, "Go and get that paper, and find the article."

When Craven returned with it, he continued, "Now, Mr. Ireland, go over those figures again; and you, Mr. Craven, check them off and see if they're correct. Now, play fair, no tricks!"

I had made two mistakes, which were reported as soon as they were spoken. At the end Mr. Pulitzer said:

"Well, you see, you hadn't got them right, after all. But that's not so bad. With a memory like that you might have known something by now if you'd only had the diligence to read."

My second score was made just at the end of dinner, or rather when dinner had been finished some time and J. P. was lingering at table over his cigar. The question of humor came up, and someone remarked how curious it was that one of the favorite amusements of the American humorist should be to make fun of the Englishman for his lack of humor - "Laugh, and all the world laughs with you, except the Englishman," and so on. The usual defenses were made - Hood, Thackeray, Gilbert, Calverley, etc. - and then Punch was referred to.

This gave me the chance of repeating, more or less accurately, a paragraph which appeared in Punch some years ago, and which I always recite when that delightful periodical is slandered in my hearing. It ran something after this fashion:

"One of our esteemed contemporaries is very much worked up in its mind about Mr. Balfour's foreign policy, which it compares to that of the camel, which, when pursued, buries its head in the sand. We quite agree with our esteemed contemporary about Mr. Balfour's foreign policy, but we fear it is getting its metaphors mixed. Surely it is not thinking of the camel which, when pursued, buries its head in the sand, but of the ostrich which, when pursued, runs its eye through a needle."

It was a lucky hit. No one had heard it before, and our party broke up with Mr. Pulitzer in high good humor.

So the days passed. I saw a great deal of Mr. Pulitzer and went through many agonizing hours of cross-examination; but gradually matters came round to the point where we discussed the possibility of my becoming a member of his personal staff. He thought that there was some hope that, if he put me through a rigorous training, I might suit him, but before it could even be settled that such an attempt should be made many things would have to be cleared up.

In the first place, I would understand what extreme caution was necessary for him in making a selection. There was not only the question of whether I could make myself useful to him, and the question of whether I could be trusted in a relationship of such a confidential nature, there remained the very important question of whether I was a fit person to associate with the lady members of his family, who spent some portion of each year with him.

This matter was discussed very frankly, and was then shelved pending a reference to a number of people in England and America at whose homes I had been a guest, and where the household included ladies.

At the end of a week the yacht was sent to Marseilles to coal in preparation for a cruise, and I went to stay at an hotel near the villa. It was a change for the worse.

By the time the yacht returned I had had some opportunity of observing the routine of life at the villa. After breakfast Mr. Pulitzer went for a drive, accompanied by one, or occasionally by two, of the secretaries. During this drive he received a rough summary of the morning's news, the papers having been gone over and marked either the night before or while he was having his breakfast.

As he seldom let us know in advance which of us he would call upon for the first presentation of the news, and as he was liable to change his mind at the last minute when he had named somebody the previous night, we had all of us to go through the papers with great care, so that we might be prepared if we were called upon.

On returning from his drive Mr. Pulitzer would either sit in the library and dictate letters and cablegrams, or he would have the news gone over in detail, or, if the state of his health forbade the mental exertion involved in the intense concentration with which he absorbed what was read to him from the papers, he would go for a ride, accompanied by a groom and by one of the secretaries. When he went to Europe he usually sent over in advance some horses from his own stable, as he was very fond of riding and could not trust himself on a strange horse.

After the ride, lunch, at which the conversation generally took a more serious turn than at dinner, for at night Mr. Pulitzer disliked any discussion of matters which were likely to arouse his interest very much or to stir his emotions, for he found it difficult to get his mind calmed down so that he could sleep. Even in regard to lunch we were sometimes warned in advance, either by Dunningham or by the secretary who had left him just before lunch was served, that Mr. Pulitzer wished the conversation to be light and uncontroversial.

Immediately after lunch Mr. Pulitzer retired to his bedroom with Herr Friederich Mann, the German secretary, and was read to, chiefly German plays, until he fell asleep, or until he had had an hour or so of rest.

By four o'clock he was ready to go out again, riding, if he had not had a ride in the morning, or driving, with an occasional walk for perhaps half-an-hour, the automobile always remaining within call. As a rule he spent an hour before dinner listening to someone read, a novel, a biography, or what not, according to his mood.

At dinner the conversation usually ran along the lines of what was being read to him by the various secretaries or of such topics in the day's news as were of an unexciting nature. The meal varied greatly in length. If J. P. was feeling tired, or out of sorts, he eat his dinner quickly and left us, taking somebody along to read to him until he was ready to go to bed. But, if he was in good form, and an interesting topic was started, or if he was in a reminiscent mood and wanted to talk, dinner would last from half-past-seven to nine, or even later.

I shall deal in another place with the different phases of the conversation and reading which formed so large a part of our duties, but I may refer here to various incidents of our routine and to some things by which our routine was occasionally disturbed.

Mr. Pulitzer was very fond of walking. His usual practice was to leave the villa in the automobile and drive either down to the plage at Mentone or up the hill to a point about midway between Cap Martin and the Tower of Augustus. When he reached the spot he had selected he took the arm of a secretary and promenaded backward and forward over a distance of five hundred yards, until he felt tired, when the automobile was signaled and we drove home.

Each of his favorite spots for walking had its peculiar disadvantages for his companion. Speaking for myself I can say that I dreaded these walks more than any other of my duties.

If we went on the hillside I had to keep the most alert and unrelaxing lookout for automobiles. They came dashing round the sharp curves with a roar and a scream, and these distracting noises always made Mr. Pulitzer stop dead still as though he were rooted to the ground.

I understand that Mr. Pulitzer was never actually hit by an automobile, and, of course, his blindness saved him from the agony of apprehension which his companion suffered, for he could not see the narrowness of his escape. But I was out with him one day on the Upper Corniche road when two automobiles going in opposite directions at reckless speed came upon us at a sharp turn, and I may frankly confess that I was never so frightened in my life. Had we been alone I am certain we would have been killed, but fortunately Mann was with us, and it was on his arm that J. P. was leaning at the critical moment. Mann, who had the advantage of long experience, acted instantly with the utmost presence of mind. He made a quick sign to me to look out for myself, and then pushed Mr. Pulitzer almost off his feet up against the high cliff which rose above the inner edge of the road.

The machines were out of sight before we could realize that we were safe. I expected an explosion from J. P. Nothing of the kind! He acted then, as I always saw him act when there was any actual danger or real trouble of any kind, with perfect calmness and self-possession.

The intolerable nervous strain of these walks on the hillside was accompanied by a mental strain almost as distressing. It would have been bad enough if one's only responsibility had been to keep Mr. Pulitzer from being crushed against the hillside, or being run over; but this was only half the problem. The other half was to keep up a continual stream of conversation - not light, airy nothings, but a solid body of carefully prepared facts - in a tone of voice which should fail to convey to J. P. the slightest indication of your nervousness.

When we walked on the plage at Mentone, the difficulties were of another kind. Here there was always more or less of a crowd, and as the paved promenade was narrow, and as very few people had the intelligence to realize that the tall, striking figure leaning on his companion's arm was that of a blind man, and as fewer still had the courtesy to step aside if they did realize it, our walk was a constant dodging in and out among curious gazers interested in staring at the gaunt, impressive invalid with the large black spectacles.

Conversation was, of course, extremely difficult under such circumstances; and occasionally things were made worse by some stranger stopping squarely in front of us and addressing Mr. Pulitzer by name, for he was a notable personage in the place and was well known by sight.

When accosted in this manner, Mr. Pulitzer always showed signs of extreme nervousness. He would stamp his foot, raise the clenched fist of his disengaged arm menacingly, and cry, "My God! What's this? What's this? Tell him to go away. I won't tolerate this intrusion. Tell him I'll have him arrested." More than once I had to push a man off the promenade and make faces at him embodying all that was possible by such means in the way of threats to do him bodily injury. It was impossible to argue with these impudent intruders, because anything like an altercation on a public road would have meant two or three days of misery for Mr. Pulitzer, in consequence of the excitement and apprehension he would suffer in such an affair. It was always with a feeling of intense relief that I saw J. P. safely back at the villa after our walks.

Although Mr. Pulitzer's intellectual interests covered almost every phase of human life, there was nothing from which he derived more pleasure than from music. Once, or perhaps twice a week, he motored over to Monte Carlo, or even as far as Nice, to attend a concert. On such occasions he always took at least two companions with him, so that he never sat next to a stranger.

He preferred a box for his party, but, failing that, the seats were always secured on the broad cross-aisle, so that he would not have to rise when anyone wished to pass in front of him. He liked to arrive a few minutes before the concert commenced, and one of us would read the program to him. He had an excellent memory for music, and his taste was broad enough to embrace almost everything good from Bach to Wagner. He was a keen critic of a performance, and in the intervals between the pieces he criticized the playing from the standpoint of his musical experience.

One movement was played too loud, another too fast; in one the brass had drowned a delightful passage for the violas, which he had heard and admired the year before in Vienna; in another the brasses had been subdued to a point where the theme lost its distinction.

It was his habit to beat time with one hand and to sway his head gently backward and forward when he heard a slow, familiar melody. When something very stirring was played, the Rakoczy March, for instance, or the overture to Die Meistersinger, he would mark the down beat with his clenched fist, and throw his head back as if he were going to shout.

I was tempted at first to believe that, in the concert room, when one of his favorite pieces was being played, and his hand rose and fell in exact accord with the conductor's baton, or when, with his head in the air and his mouth half open, he thumped his knee at the beginning of each bar, he was absorbed in the music to the exclusion of all his worries, perplexities, and suffering.

But, after he had once or twice turned to me in a flash as the last note of a symphony lingered before the outburst of applause and asked, "Did you remember to tell Dunningham to have dinner served a quarter of an hour later this evening?" or "Did Thwaites say anything to you about when he expected those cables from New York?" - I learned that even at such times J. P. never lost the thread of his existence, never freed himself from the slavery of his affairs.

Twice during the ten days immediately preceding our long promised cruise in the Mediterranean we made short trips on the yacht. We went to bed some nights with all our plans apparently settled for a week ahead. At eight o'clock the next morning Dunningham would bring J. P. down to breakfast and then announce that everybody was to be on board the yacht by midday, as J. P. had slept badly and felt the need of sea air and the complete quiet which could be had only on board the Liberty.

There would be a great packing of trunks, not only those devoted to the personal belongings of the staff, but trunks for newspaper files, encyclopedias, magazines, novels, histories, correspondence, and so on.

The chef and his assistants, the butler and his assistants, the major domo, and the secretaries would leave the villa in a string of carriages, followed by cartloads of baggage, and install themselves on the yacht.

Or the cause of our sudden departure might be that Mr. Pulitzer was feeling nervous and out of sorts and was expecting important letters or cables which were sure to excite him and make him worse. On such occasions Dunningham, who was one of the few people who had any influence whatever over Mr. Pulitzer, would urge an instant flight on the yacht as the only means of safeguarding J. P.'s health. He knew that if we stayed ashore no power on earth could prevent Mr. Pulitzer from reading his cables and letters when they arrived. Once out at sea we were completely cut off from communication with the shore, for we had no wireless apparatus, and Mr. Pulitzer would settle down and get some rest.

More than once, however, I saw all the preparations made for a short cruise, everybody on board, the captain on the bridge, the table laid for lunch, a man stationed at the stem to report the automobile as soon as it came in sight, and at the last moment a messenger arrive countermanding everything and ordering everybody back to the villa as fast as they could go.

These sudden changes were sometimes reversed. We would arrive at Mentone in the morning. J. P. would announce his intention of spending a week there. With this apparently settled, J. P. goes ashore for a ride, the procession makes its way to the villa, the trunks are unpacked, the chef begins to ply his art, the captain of the yacht goes ahead with such washing down and painting as are needed, the chief engineer seizes the chance of making some small engine-room repairs - no ordinary ship's work of any kind was allowed when J. P. was on board, the slightest noise or the faintest odor of paint being strictly forbidden - and later in the day the news comes that Mr. Pulitzer will be aboard again in two hours and will expect everything to be ready to make an immediate start.

These short cruises might last only for a night, or they might extend to a day or two, Our custom was to steam straight out to sea and then patrol the coast backward and forward between Bordighera and Cannes, without losing sight of land.

The life at Cap Martin was sufficiently arduous, even for those who had after long experience with J. P. learned to get through the day with some economy of effort. To me, new to the work, constantly under the double pressure of Mr. Pulitzer's cross-examinations and of the task of supplying, however inefficiently, the place of a secretary who was away on sick leave, the whole thing was a nightmare. I was in a dazed condition; everything impressed itself upon me with the vividness of a dream, and eluded my attempts at analysis, just as the delusive order of our sleeping visions breaks up into topsyturvydom as soon as we try to reconstruct it in the light of day.

I spent in all about a month at Cap Martin, staying sometimes on the yacht and sometimes at an hotel, and during that time I worked practically every day from eight in the morning until ten or eleven at night. I use the word "work" to include the hours spent with Mr. Pulitzer as well as those devoted to preparing material for him. Indeed, the time given to meals and to drives and walks with J. P. was much more exhausting than that spent in reading and in making notes.

The only recreation I had during this period was one day on leave at Nice and half a day at Monaco; but there was very little enjoyment to be got out of these visits, because I was under orders to bring back minute descriptions of Nice and of the Institute of Marine Biology at Monaco.

Engaged on such missions, the passers-by, the houses, the shops, the fishes and marine vegetables in their tanks, the blue sky overhead, the blue sea at my feet assumed a new aspect to me. They were no longer parts of my own observation, to be remembered or forgotten as chance determined, they belonged to some one else, to the blind man in whose service I was pledged to a vicarious absorption of "material."

I found myself counting the black spots on a fish's back, the steps leading up to Monaco on its hill, the number of men and women in the Grand Salon at Monte Carlo, of men with mustaches, of clean-shaven men, of men with beards in the restaurants, of vessels in sight from the terrace, of everything, in fact, which seemed capable of furnishing a sentence or of starting up a discussion.

Once or twice I ran over late at night to Monte Carlo, and occasionally Thwaites and I met after ten o'clock at the Casino of Mentone to play bowls or try our luck at the tables; but the spirit of J. P. never failed to attend upon these dismal efforts at amusement. If I heard an epigram, witnessed an interesting incident, or observed any curious sight, out came my note book and pencil and the matter was dedicated to the service of the morrow's duties.

Finally, after several false starts, we all found ourselves on the yacht with the prospect of spending most of our time aboard until Mr. Pulitzer sailed for his annual visit to America.

CHAPTER IV

YACHTING IN THE MEDITERRANEAN

Taken at its face value a month in the Mediterranean, on board one of the finest yachts afloat, with visits to Corsica, Elba, Nice, Cannes, Naples, Genoa, Syracuse, and the Pirams, should give promise of a picturesque and entertaining record of sight-seeing, the kind of journal in which the views of Baedeker and of your local cab driver are blended, in order that the aroma of foreign travel may be wafted to the nostrils of your fresh-water cousins.

What my narrative lacks of this flavor of luxurious vagrancy must be supplied by the peculiar interest of a cruise which violated every tradition of the annals of yachting, and created precedents which in all human probability will never be followed so long as iron floats on water.

It was part of Mr. Pulitzer's scheme of nautical life to shroud all his movements in mystery. One result of this was that when we were on the yacht we never knew where we were going until we got there. The compass-course at any moment betrayed nothing of Mr. Pulitzer's intentions, for we might turn in at night with the ship heading straight for Naples and wake up in the morning to find ourselves three miles south of the Genoa lighthouse.

Apart from Mr. Pulitzer's fancy, our erratic maneuvers were affected by our need to make good weather out of whatever wind we encountered, on the one hand because J. P., though an excellent sailor, disliked the rolling produced by a beam sea, since it interfered with his walking on deck, and on the other hand, because several of the secretaries suffered from sea-sickness the moment we were off an even keel.

Mr. Pulitzer was not a man prone to be placated by excuses; but he had come to realize that neither a sense of duty nor the hope of reward, neither fear nor courage, can make an agreeable companion out of a man who is seasick. So, unless there was an important reason why we should reach port, we always made a head-wind of anything stronger than a light breeze, and followed the weather round the compass until it was fair for our destination.

As soon as we left Mentone Mr. Pulitzer began the process of education which was designed to fit me for his service.

"When you were in New York," he asked, "what papers did you read?"

"The Sun and The Times in the morning and The Evening Sun and The Evening Post at night," I replied.

"My God! Didn't you read The World?"

"Nothing but the editorial page."

"Why not? What's the matter with it?"

I explained that I was not interested in crime and disaster, to which The World devoted so much space, that I wanted more foreign news than The World found room for, and that I was offended by the big headlines, which compelled me to know things I didn't want to know.

"Go on," he said; "your views are not of any importance, but they're entertaining."

"Well," I continued, "I think The World was excellently described a few years ago in Life. There was a poem entitled, 'New York Newspaper Directory, Revised,' in which a verse was devoted to each of the big New York papers. I believe I can remember the one about The World, if you care to hear it, for I cut the poem out and have kept it among my clippings."

"Certainly, go ahead."

I recited:

> "A dual personality is this,
> Part yellow dog, part patriot and sage;
> When't comes to facts the rule is hit or miss,
> While none can beat its editorial page.
> Wise counsel here, wild yarns the other side,
> Page six its Jekyll and page one its Hyde;
> At the same time conservative and rash,
> The World supplies us good advice and trash."

"That's clever," said Mr. Pulitzer, "but it's absolute nonsense, except about the editorial page. Have you got the clipping with you? I would like to hear what that smart young man has got to say about the other papers."

I went to my cabin, got the poem, and read the whole of it to him - witty characterizations of The Evening Post, The Sun, The Journal, The Tribune, The Times and The Herald. As soon as I had finished reading, Mr. Pulitzer said:

"The man who wrote those verses had his prejudices, but he was clever. I'm glad you read them to me; always read me anything of that kind, anything that is bright and satirical. Now, I'm going to give you a lecture about newspapers, because I want you to understand my point of view. It does not matter whether you agree with it or not, but you have got to understand it if you are going to be of any use to me. But before I begin, you tell me what YOUR ideas are about running a newspaper for American readers."

I pleaded that I had never given the matter much thought, and that I had little to guide me, except my own preferences and the memory of an occasional discussion here and there at a club or in the smoking room of a Pullman. He insisted, however, and so I launched forth upon a discourse in regard to the functions, duties and responsibilities of an American newspaper, as I imagined they would appear to the average American reader.

The chief duty of a managing editor, I said, was to give his readers an interesting paper, and as an angler baits his hook, not with what HE likes, but with what the fish like, so the style of the newspaper should be adjusted to what the managing editor judged to be the public appetite.

A sub-stratum of truth should run through the news columns; but since a million-dollar fire is more exciting than a half-million-dollar fire, since a thousand deaths in an earthquake are more exciting than a hundred, no nice scrupulosity need be observed in checking the insurance inspector's figures or in counting the dead. What the public wanted was a good "story," and provided it got that there would be little disposition in any quarter to censure an arithmetical generosity which had been invoked in the service of the public's well-known demands.

So far as politics were concerned, it seemed to me that any newspaper could afford the strongest support to its views while printing the truth and nothing but the truth, if it exercised some discretion as to printing the WHOLE truth. The editorial, I added, might be regarded as a habit rather than as a guiding force. People no longer looked to the editorial columns for the formation of their opinions. They formed their judgment from a large stock of facts, near-facts and nowhere near-facts, and then bought a paper for the purpose of comfortable reassurance. I had no doubt that a newspaper run to suit my own taste - a combination of The World's editorial page with The Evening Post's news and make-up - would lack the influence with which circulation alone can endow a paper, and would end in a bankruptcy highly creditable to its stockholders.

This somewhat cynical outburst brought down upon me an overwhelming torrent of protest from Mr. Pulitzer.

"My God!" he cried, "I would not have believed it possible that any one could show such a complete ignorance of American character, of the high sense of duty which in the main animates American journalism, of the foundations of integrity on which almost every successful paper in the United States has been founded. You do not know what it costs me to try and keep The World up to a high standard of accuracy - the money, the time, the thought, the praise, the blame, the constant watchfulness.

"I do not say that The World never makes a mistake in its news column; I wish I could say it. What I say is that there are not half a dozen papers in the United States which tamper with the news, which publish what they know to be false. But if I thought that I had done no better than that I would be ashamed to own a paper. It is not enough to refrain from publishing fake news, it is not enough to take ordinary care to avoid the mistakes which arise from the ignorance, the carelessness, the stupidity of one or more of the many men who handle the news before it gets into print; you have got to do much more than that; you have got to make every one connected with the paper - your editors, your reporters, your correspondents, your rewrite men, your proof-readers - believe that accuracy is to a newspaper what virtue is to a woman.

"When you go to New York ask any of the men in the dome to show you my instructions to them, my letters written from day to day, my cables; and you will see that accuracy, accuracy, accuracy, is the first, the most urgent, the most constant demand I have made on them.

"I do not say that The World is the only paper which takes extraordinary pains to be accurate; on the contrary, I think that almost every paper in America tries to be accurate. I will go further than that. There is not a paper of any importance published in French, German or English, whether it is printed in Europe or in America, which I have not studied for weeks or months, and some of them I have read steadily for a quarter of a century; and I tell you this, Mr. Ireland, after years of experience, after having comparisons made by the hundred, from time to time, of different versions of the same event, that the press of America as a whole has a higher standard of accuracy than the European press as a whole. I will go further than that. I will say that line for line the American newspapers actually ATTAIN a higher standard of news accuracy than the European newspapers; and I will go further than that and say that although there are in Europe a few newspapers, and they are chiefly English, which are as accurate as the best newspapers in America, there are no newspapers in America which are so habitually, so criminally stuffed with fake news as the worst of the European papers."

Mr. Pulitzer paused and asked me if there was a glass of water on the table - we were seated in his library - and after I had handed it to him and he had drained it nearly to the bottom at one gulp, he resumed his lecture. I give it in considerable detail, because it was the longest speech he ever addressed to me, because he subsequently made me write it out from memory and then read it to him, and because it was one of the few occasions during my intercourse with him on which I was persuaded beyond a doubt that he spoke with perfect frankness, without allowing his words to be influenced by any outside considerations.

"As a matter of fact," he continued, "the criticisms you hear about the American press are founded on a dislike for our headlines and for the prominence we give to crime, to corruption in office, and to sensational topics generally; the charge of inaccuracy is just thrown in to make it look worse. I do not believe that one person in a thousand who attacks the American press for being inaccurate has ever taken the trouble to investigate the facts.

Alleyne Ireland

"Now about this matter of sensationalism: a newspaper should be scrupulously accurate, it should be clean, it should avoid everything salacious or suggestive, everything that could offend good taste or lower the moral tone of its readers; but within these limits it is the duty of a newspaper to print the news. When I speak of good taste and of good moral tone I do not mean the kind of good taste which is offended by every reference to the unpleasant things of life, I do not mean the kind of morality which refuses to recognize the existence of immorality - that type of moral hypocrite has done more to check the moral progress of humanity than all the immoral people put together - what I mean is the kind of good taste which demands that frankness should be linked with decency, the kind of moral tone which is braced and not relaxed when it is brought face to face with vice.

"Some people try and make you believe that a newspaper should not devote its space to long and dramatic accounts of murders, railroad wrecks, fires, lynchings, political corruption, embezzlements, frauds, graft, divorces, what you will. I tell you they are wrong, and I believe that if they thought the thing out they would see that they are wrong.

"We are a democracy, and there is only one way to get a democracy on its feet in the matter of its individual, its social, its municipal, its State, its National conduct, and that is by keeping the public informed about what is going on. There is not a crime, there is not a dodge, there is not a trick, there is not a swindle, there is not a vice which does not live by secrecy. Get these things out in the open, describe them, attack them, ridicule them in the press, and sooner or later public opinion will sweep them away.

"Publicity may not be the only thing that is needed, but it is the one thing without which all other agencies will fail. If a newspaper is to be of real service to the public it must have a big circulation, first because its news and its comment must reach the largest possible number of people, second, because circulation means advertising, and advertising means money, and money means independence. If I caught any man on The World suppressing news because one of our advertisers objected to having it printed I would dismiss him immediately; I wouldn't care who he was.

"What a newspaper needs in its news, in its headlines, and on its editorial page is terseness, humor, descriptive power, satire, originality, good literary style, clever condensation, and accuracy, accuracy, accuracy!"

Mr. Pulitzer made this confession of faith with the warmth generated by an unshakable faith. He spoke, as he always spoke when he was excited, with vigor, emphasis and ample gesture. When he came to an end and asked for another glass of water I found nothing to say. It would have been as impertinent of me to agree with him as to differ from him.

After all, I had to remember that he had taken over The World when its circulation was less than 15,000 copies a day; that he had been for thirty years and still was its dominating spirit and the final authority on every matter concerning its policy, its style, and its contents; that he had seen its morning circulation go up to well over 350,000 copies a day; that at times he had taken his stand boldly against popular clamor, as when he kept up for months a bitter attack against the American action in the Venezuelan boundary dispute, and at times had incurred the hostility of powerful moneyed interests, as when he forced the Cleveland administration to sell to the public on competitive bids a fifty-million-dollar bond issue which it had arranged to sell privately to a great banking house at much less than its market value.

Before leaving the subject of newspapers I may describe the method by which Mr. Pulitzer kept in touch with the news and put himself in the position to maintain a critical supervision over The World.

An elaborate organization was employed for this purpose. I will explain it as it worked when we were on the yacht, but the system was maintained at all times, whether we were cruising, or were at Cap Martin, at Bar Harbor, at Wiesbaden, or elsewhere, merely a few minor details being changed to meet local conditions.

In the Pulitzer Building, Park Row, New York, there were collected each day several copies of each of the morning papers, including The World, and some of the evening papers. These were mailed daily to Mr. Pulitzer according to cabled instructions as to our whereabouts. In addition to this a gentleman connected with The World, who had long experience of Mr. Pulitzer's requirements, cut from all the New York papers and from a number of other papers from every part of the United States every article that he considered Mr. Pulitzer ought to see, whether because of its subject, its tenor, or its style. These clippings were mailed by the hundred on almost every fast steamer sailing for Europe. In order that there might be the greatest economy of time in reading them, the essential matter in each clipping was marked.

So far as The World was concerned a copy of each issue was sent, with the names of the writers written across each editorial, big news story, or special article.

As we went from port to port we got the principal French, German, Austrian and Italian papers, and The World bureau in London kept us supplied with the English dailies and weeklies.

Whenever we picked up a batch of American papers, each of the secretaries got a set and immediately began to read it. My own method of reading was adopted after much advice from Mr. Pulitzer and after consultation with the more experienced members of the staff, and I do not suppose it differed materially from that followed by the others.

I read The World first, going over the "big" stories carefully and with enough concentration to give me a very fair idea of the facts. Then I read the articles in the other papers covering the same ground, noting any important differences in the various accounts. This task resolved itself in practice into mastering in considerable detail about half a dozen articles - a political situation, a murder, a railroad wreck, a fire, a strike, an important address by a college president, for example - and getting a clear impression of the treatment of each item in each paper.

With this done, and with a few notes scribbled on a card to help my memory, I turned to the editorial pages, reading each editorial with the closest attention, and making more notes.

The final reading of the news served to give me from ten to twenty small topics of what Mr. Pulitzer called "human interest," to be used as subjects of conversation as occasion demanded. As a rule, I cut these items out of the paper and put them in the left-hand pocket of my coat, for when we walked together J. P. always took my right arm, and my left hand was therefore free to dip into my reservoir of cuttings whenever conversation flagged and I needed a new subject.

The cuttings covered every imaginable topic - small cases in the magistrates' courts, eccentric entertainments at Newport, the deaths of centenarians, dinners to visiting authors in New York, accounts of performing animals, infant prodigies, new inventions, additions to the Metropolitan Museum, announcements of new plays, anecdotes about prominent men and women, instances of foolish extravagance among the rich, and so on.

Something of the kind was done by each of us, so that when Mr. Pulitzer appeared on deck after breakfast we all had something ready for him. The first man called usually had the easiest time, for Mr. Pulitzer's mind was fresh and keen for news after a night's rest. The men who went to him later in the morning suffered from two disadvantages, one that they did not know what news or how much of it J. P. had already received, the other that as the day advanced Mr. Pulitzer often grew tired, and his attention then became difficult to hold.

I remember that on one occasion when he had complained of feeling utterly tired out mentally I asked him if he would like me to stop talking. "No, no," he replied at once; "never stop talking or reading, I must have something to occupy my mind all the time, however exhausted I am."

This peculiarity of being unable to get any repose by the road of silent abstraction must have been a source of acute suffering to him. It is difficult to imagine a more terrible condition of mind than that in which the constant flogging of a tired brain is the only anodyne for its morbid irritability.

My own experience of a morning on the yacht, when Mr. Pulitzer's nerves had been soothed by a good night's sleep, was that he walked up and down the long promenade deck and got from me a brief summary of the news.

From time to time he pulled out his watch and, holding it toward me, asked what o'clock it was. He was always most particular to know exactly how long he had walked. We had arguments on many occasions as to the exact moment at which we had commenced our promenade, and we would go carefully over the facts - Mr. Craven had been walking with him from 9.30 to 10.05, then Dunningham had been in the library with him for fifteen minutes, then Mr. Thwaites had walked with him for ten minutes, taking notes for a letter to be written to the managing editor of The World; well, that made it 10.30 when I joined him; but fifteen minutes had to be taken out of the hour for the time he'd spent in the library, that made three-quarters of an hour he'd been actually walking, well, we'd walk for another fifteen minutes and round out the hour.

Often when the appointed moment came to stop walking Mr. Pulitzer felt able to go on, and he would then either say frankly, "Let's have fifteen minutes more," or he would achieve the same end by reopening the discussion as to just how long he had walked, and keep on walking until he began to feel tired, when he would say: "I dare say you are quite right, well, now we will sit down and go over the papers."

The question of where Mr. Pulitzer was to sit on deck was not a simple one to decide. He always wanted as much air as he could get; but as he suffered a good deal of pain in his right eye, the one which had been operated on, and as this was either started or made worse by exposure to wind, a spot had to be found which had just the right amount of air current. Five minutes might show, however, that there was a little too much wind, when we would move to a more sheltered spot, or he might think we'd been too cautious and that he could sit in a breezier spot, or, after we had found the ideal place, the wind might change, and then we had to move again.

Settled in a large cane armchair with a leather seat, a heavy rug over his knees if the weather was at all chilly, Mr. Pulitzer took up the serious consideration of the news which had been lightly skimmed over during his walk.

An item was selected, and the account in The World was read aloud. Then followed the discussion of it from the standpoint of its presentation in the various papers. On what page was it printed in The World, in what column, how much space did it fill, how much was devoted to headlines, what was the size of the type, was the type varied in parts to give emphasis to the more striking features of the story, what were the cross-heads in the body of the article, were any boxes used, if so, what was put in them, what about the illustrations? And so on for each important item in each paper.

One of the by-products of this reading of the papers was a stream of cables, letters and memoranda to various members of The World staff in New York. None of these were ever sent through me, but it was a common thing for J. P. to say: "Have you got your writing pad with you? Just make a note: Indianapolis story excellent, insufficient details lynching, who wrote City Hall story? and give it to Thwaites and tell him to remind me of it this afternoon."

Mr. Pulitzer would take the matter up with Thwaites, and would send such praise, blame, reward, criticism, or suggestion as the occasion demanded.

From time to time I was called upon to make a report on the day's papers, a task which usually fell to some more experienced member of the staff. My reports always covered the Sunday issues. They included an analysis of The Sun, The Herald, The American, The Times, The Tribune and The World, showing the number of columns of advertising, of news, and of special articles, a classification of the telegrams according to geographical distribution - how much from France, from Germany, from England, from the Western States, from the Southern States, and so on; a classification of the special articles on the basis of their topics - medicine, sport, fashions, humor, adventure, children's interests, women's interests.

This was by no means the only check which Mr. Pulitzer kept upon The World and its contemporaries. He received regularly from New York a statistical return showing, for The World and its two principal competitors, the monthly and yearly figures for circulation and advertising; and the advertising return showed not only the amount of space occupied by advertising in each paper, but also the number of advertisements each month under various heads, such as display advertising, want ads., real estate, dry goods, amusements, hotels, transportation, to let ads., summer resorts, and whatever other classes of advertising might appear.

Whatever Mr. Pulitzer wished to do in the way of business, whether it concerned the direction of the policy of The World, or the dictating of an editorial, or the handling of correspondence, was almost always done in the morning, and by lunch time he was ready to turn his attention to something light or amusing, or to serious subjects not connected with current events.

Mr. Pulitzer generally lunched and dined with the staff in the dining saloon, unless he felt more than usually ill or nervous, when he had his meals served in the library, one or at most two of us keeping him company.

When he sat with us he occupied the head of the table. At his side stood the butler, who never attended to any one but his master. A stranger at the table, if he were not actually sitting next to J. P., might very well have failed to notice that his host was blind, so far as any indication of blindness was afforded by the way he ate. His food was, of course, cut up at a side table, but it was placed before him on an ordinary plate, without any raised edge or other device to save it from being pushed on to the tablecloth.

As soon as he was seated J. P. put his fingers lightly on the table in front of him and fixed the exact position of his plate, fork, spoon, water glass and wine glass. While he was doing this he generally spoke a few words to one or another of us, and as he always turned his face in the direction of the person he was addressing, the delicate movements of his hands, even if they were observed, were only those of a man with his sight under similar circumstances.

Sitting next to him, however, his blindness soon became apparent. As he began to eat he simply impaled each portion of food on his fork, but after he had got halfway through a course and the remaining morsels were scattered here and there on his plate, he explored the surface with the utmost niceness of touch until he felt a slight resistance. He had then located a morsel, but in order that he might avoid an accident in transferring it to his mouth he felt the object carefully all over with almost imperceptible touches of his fork, and, having found the thickest or firmest part of it secured it safely.

At times, if he became particularly interested in the conversation, he put his fork down, and when he picked it up again he was in difficulties for a moment or two, having lost track of the food remaining on his plate. On these occasions the ever-watchful butler would either place the food with a fork in the track of J. P.'s systematic exploration, or guide Mr. Pulitzer's hand to the right spot.

Like many people in broken health Mr. Pulitzer had a very variable appetite. Sometimes nothing could tempt his palate, sometimes he ate voraciously; but at all times the greatest care had to be exercised in regard to his diet. Not only did he suffer constantly from acute dyspepsia, but also from diabetes, which varied in sympathy with his general state of health.

He took very little alcohol, and that only in the form of light wines, such as claret or hock, seldom more than a single small glass at lunch and at dinner. Whenever he found a vintage which specially appealed to him he would tell the butler to send a case or two to some old friend in America, to some member of his family or to one of the staff of The World.

After lunch Mr. Pulitzer always retired to his cabin for a siesta. I use the word siesta, but as a matter of fact it is quite inadequate to describe the peculiar function for which I have chosen it as a label. What took place on these occasions was this: Mr. Pulitzer lay down on his bed, sometimes in pyjamas, but more often with only his coat and boots removed, and one of the secretaries, usually the German secretary, sat down in an armchair at the bedside with a pile of books at his elbow.

At a word from Mr. Pulitzer the secretary began to read in a clear, incisive voice some historical work, novel or play. After a few minutes Mr. Pulitzer would say "Softly," and the secretary's voice was lowered until, though it was still audible, it assumed a monotonous and soothing quality. After a while the order came, "Quite softly." At this point the reader ceased to form his words and commenced to murmur indistinctly, giving an effect such as might be produced by a person reading aloud in an adjoining room, but with the connecting door closed.

If, after ten minutes of this murmuring, J. P. remained motionless it was to be assumed that he was asleep; and the secretary's duty was to go on murmuring until Mr. Pulitzer awoke and told him to stop or to commence actual reading again. This murmuring might last for two hours, and it was a very difficult art to acquire, for at the slightest change in the pitch of the voice, at a sneeze, or a cough, Mr. Pulitzer would wake with a start, and an unpleasant quarter of an hour followed.

This murmuring was not, however, without its consolations to the murmurer, for as soon as the actual reading stopped he could take up a novel or magazine and, leaving his vocal organs to carry on the work, concentrate his mind upon the preparation of material against some future session.

The siesta over, the afternoon was taken up with much the same kind of work as had filled the morning. By six o'clock Mr. Pulitzer was ready to sit in the library for an hour before he dressed for dinner. This time was generally devoted to novels, plays and light literature of various kinds. J. P. often assured me that no man had ever been able to read a novel or a play to him satisfactorily without having first gone over it carefully at least twice; and on more than one occasion I was furnished with very good evidence that even this double preparation was not always a guarantee of success.

There appeared to be two ways of getting Mr. Pulitzer interested in a novel or play. One, and this, I believe, was the most successful, was to draw a striking picture of the scene where the climax is reached - the wife crouching in the corner, the husband revolver in hand, the Tertium Quid calmly offering to read the documents which prove that he and not the gentleman with the revolver is really the husband of the lady - and then to go back to the beginning and explain how it all came about.

The other method was to set forth the appearance and disposition of each of the characters in the story, so that they assumed reality in Mr. Pulitzer's mind, then to condense the narrative up to about page two hundred and sixty, and then begin to read from the book. If in the course of the next three minutes you were not asked in a tone of utter weariness, "My God! Is there much more of this?" there was a reasonable chance that you might be allowed to read from the print a fifth or possibly a fourth of what you had not summarized.

Dinner on the yacht passed in much the same way as lunch, except that serious subjects and especially politics were taboo.

The meal hours were really the most trying experiences of the day. Each of us went to the table with several topics of conversation carefully prepared, with our pockets full of newspaper cuttings, notes and even small reference books for dates and biographies.

But there was seldom any conversation in the proper sense; that is to say, we were hardly ever able to start a subject going and pass it from one to the other with a running comment or amplification, partly because any expression of opinion, except when he, J. P., asked for it, usually bored him to extinction, and partly because the first statement of any striking fact generally inspired Mr. Pulitzer to undertake a searching cross-examination of the speaker into every detail of the matter brought forward, and in regard to every ramification of the subject.

I may relate an amusing instance of this: A gentleman who had been on the staff, but had been absent through illness, joined us at Mentone for a cruise in the Eastern Mediterranean. At dinner the first night out he incautiously mentioned that during the two months of his convalescence he had taken the opportunity of reading the whole of Shakespeare's plays.

Too late he realized his mistake. Mr. Pulitzer took the matter up, and for the next hour and a half we listened to the unfortunate ex-invalid while he gave a list of the principal characters in each of the historical plays, in each of the tragedies, and in each of the comedies, followed by an outline of each plot, a description of a scene here and there, and an occasional quotation from the text.

At the end of this heroic exploit, which was helped out now and then by a note from one of the rest of us, scribbled hastily on a card and handed silently to the victim, Mr. Pulitzer merely said, "Well, go on, go on, didn't you read the sonnets?" But this was too much for our gravity, and in a ripple of laughter the sitting was brought to a close.

The trouble with the meals, however, was not only that we were all kept at a very high strain of alertness and attention, singularly inconducive to the enjoyment of food or to the sober business of digestion, but that they were of such interminable length. The plain fact was that by utilizing almost every moment between eight o'clock in the morning and nine o'clock at night we could fortify ourselves with enough material to fill in the hour or two spent with Mr. Pulitzer, hours during which we had to supply an incessant stream of information, or run through a carefully condensed novel or play.

Under such circumstances an hour for lunch or dinner had to be accepted as an unfortunate necessity; but when it came, as it often did, to an hour and a half or two hours, the encroachment on our time became a serious matter.

At about nine o'clock Mr. Pulitzer went to the library. One of the secretaries accompanied him and read aloud until, on the stroke of ten, Dunningham came and announced that it was bedtime.

An extraordinary, and in some respects a most annoying feature of this final task of the day, viewed from the secretary's standpoint, was that from nine to ten, almost without cessation, Mr. Mann, the German secretary, played the piano in the dining saloon, the doors communicating with the library being left open.

In a direct line the piano cannot have been more than ten feet from the reader's chair; and the strain of reading aloud for an hour against a powerful rendering of the most vigorous compositions of Liszt, Wagner, Beethoven, Brahms and Chopin was a most trying ordeal for voice, brain and nerves. Mr. Pulitzer could apparently enjoy the music and the reading at the same time. Often, when something was played of which he knew the air, he would follow the notes by means of a sort of subdued whistle, beating time with his hand; but this did not take his mind off the reading, and if you allowed your attention to wander for a moment and failed to read with proper emphasis he would say: "Please read that last passage over again, and do try and read it distinctly."

Such was the routine of life on the yacht. It was little affected by our occasional visits to Naples, Ajaccio and other ports. Some one always landed to inquire for mail and to procure newspapers, one or two of us got shore leave for a few hours, but so far as I was concerned, being still in strict training and under close observation, my rare landings were made only for the purpose of having my observation and memory tested.

I brought back minute descriptions of Napoleon's birthplace at Ajaccio, of his villa in Elba, of the tapestries, pictures and statues in the National Museum at Naples, of the Acropolis, of the monument of Lysicrates, of the Greek Theater and of the Roman Amphitheater at Syracuse, and of whatever else I was directed to observe.

Mr. Pulitzer had had these things described to him a score of times. He knew which block of seats in the Greek theater at Neapolis bore the inscription of Nereis, daughter-in-law of King Heiro the Second; he knew up what stairs and through what rooms and passages you had to go to see the marble bath in Napoleon's villa near Portoferraio; he knew from precisely what part of the Acropolis the yacht was visible when it was at anchor at the Piraeus; he knew the actual place of the more important pictures on the walls of each room of the Naples Museum - such a one to the right, such a one to the left as you entered - he knew practically everything, but specially he knew the thing you had forgotten.

My exhibitions of memory always ended, as they were no doubt intended to end, in a confession of ignorance. If I described five pictures, Mr. Pulitzer said: "Go on"; when I had described ten, he said: "Go on"; when I had described fifteen he said: "Go on"; and this was kept up until I could go on no more. At this point Mr. Pulitzer had discovered just what he wanted to know - how much I could see in a given time, and how much of it I could remember with a fair degree of accuracy. It was simply the game of the jewels which Lurgan Sahib played with Kim, against a different background but with much the same object.

In the foregoing description of Mr. Pulitzer's daily life it has been made abundantly clear that his secretaries were worked to the limit of their endurance. It remains to add that Mr. Pulitzer never made a demand upon us which was greater than the demand he made upon himself.

He was a tremendous worker; and in receiving our reports no vital fact ever escaped him. If we missed one he immediately "sensed" it, and his untiring cross-examination clung to the trail until he unearthed it.

We had youth, health and numbers on our side, yet this man, aged by suffering, tormented by ill-health, loaded with responsibility, kept pace with our united labors, and in the final analysis gave more than he received.

We brought a thousand offerings to his judgment; many of them he rejected with an impatient cry of "Next! Next! For God's sake!" But if any subject, whether from its intrinsic importance or from its style, reached the standard of his discrimination he took it up, enlarged upon it, illuminated it, until what had come to him as crude material for conversation assumed a new form, everything unessential rejected, every-thing essential disclosed in the clear and vigorous English which was the vehicle of his lucid thought.

When I recall the capaciousness of his understanding, the breadth of his experience, the range of his information, and set them side by side with the cruel limitations imposed upon him by his blindness and by his shattered constitution, I forget the severity of his discipline, I marvel only that his self-control should have served him so well in the tedious business of breaking a new man to his service.

CHAPTER V

GETTING TO KNOW MR. PULITZER

As time passed, my relations with Mr. Pulitzer became more agreeable. He had given me fair warning that the first few weeks of my trial would be more or less unpleasant; a month at Cap Martin and a month on the yacht had amply verified his prediction.

But this period of probation, laborious and nerve-racking as it was, enabled me to appreciate how important it was for J. P. to put to a severe test of ability, tact and good temper any one whom he intended to attach to his personal staff.

His total blindness placed him completely in the hands of those around him, and, in order that he might enjoy that sense of perfect security without which his life would have been intolerable, it was necessary that he should be able to repose absolute confidence in the loyalty and intelligence of his companions.

It was not with reference to his blindness alone that the qualifications of his secretaries were measured. Indeed, to the loss of his sight he had become, in some measure, reconciled; what really dominated every other consideration was the need of being able to meet the peculiar conditions which had arisen through the complete breakdown of his nervous system.

I have spoken of his extreme sensitiveness to noise. It is

impossible to give any description of this terrible symptom which shall be in any way adequate. Many of us suffer torment through the hideous clamor which appears to be inseparable from modern civilization; but to Mr. Pulitzer even the sudden click of a spoon against a saucer, the gurgle of water poured into a glass, the striking of a match, produced a spasm of suffering. I have seen him turn pale, tremble, break into a cold perspiration at some sound which to most people would have been scarcely audible.

When we were on the yacht every one was compelled to wear rubber-soled shoes. When Mr. Pulitzer was asleep that portion of the deck which was over his bedroom was roped off so that no one could walk over his head; and each door which gave access to the rooms above his cabin was provided with a brass plate on which was cut the legend: "This door must not be opened when Mr. Pulitzer is asleep."

With every resource at his command which ingenuity could suggest and money procure, the one great unsolved problem of his later years was to obtain absolute quietness at all times. At his magnificent house in New York, at his beautiful country home at Bar Harbor he had spent tens of thousands of dollars in a vain effort to procure the one luxury which he prized above all others. On the yacht the conditions in this respect were as nearly perfect as possible; but some noise was inseparable from the ship's work - letting go the anchor, heaving it up again, blowing the foghorn, and so on - though most of the ordinary noises had been eliminated.

As an instance of the constant care which was taken to save Mr. Pulitzer from noise I remember that for some days almonds were served with our dessert at dinner, but that they suddenly ceased to form part of our menu. Being fond of almonds, I asked the chief steward why they had stopped serving them. After a little hesitation he said that it had been done at the suggestion of the butler, who had noticed that I broke the almonds in half before I ate them and that the noise made by their snapping was very disagreeable to Mr. Pulitzer.

With the best intentions in the world, our meals were now and then disturbed by noise. A knife suddenly slipped with a loud click against a plate, a waiter dropped a spoon on a silver tray, or some one knocked over a glass. We were all in such a state of nervous tension that whenever one of these little accidents occurred we jumped in our chairs as though a pistol had been fired, and looked at J. P. with horrified expectancy.

There could be no doubt whatever as to the effect these noises had upon him. He winced as a dog winces when you crack a whip over him; the only question was whether by a powerful effort he could regain his composure or whether his suffering would overcome his self-restraint to the extent of making him gloomy or querulous during the rest of the meal.

The effect by no means ceased when we rose from table. If by bad luck two or three noises occurred at dinner - and our excessive anxiety in the matter was sometimes our undoing - Mr. Pulitzer was so upset that he would pass a sleepless night. This in its turn meant a day during which his tortured body made itself master of his mind, and plunged him into a state of profound dejection.

Like most people who suffer acutely from noise Mr. Pulitzer was very differently affected by different kinds of noise. To any noise which was necessary, such as that caused by letting go the anchor, he could make himself indifferent; but very few noises were included in this category.

What caused him the most acute suffering was a noise which, while it inflicted pain upon him, neither gave pleasure to any one else nor achieved a useful purpose. Loud talking, whistling, slamming doors, carelessness in handling things, the barking of dogs, the "kick" of motor boats, these were the noises which made his existence miserable.

At the back of his physical reaction was a mental reaction which intensified every shock to his nerves. He complained, and with justice, that, leaving out of consideration an occasional noise which was purely the result of accident, his life was made a burden by the utter indifference of the majority of human beings to the rights of others. What right, he asked, had any one to run a motor boat with a machine so noisy that it destroyed the peace of a whole harbor? Above all, what right had such a person to come miles out to sea and cruise around the yacht, merely to gratify idle curiosity?

He applied the same test to people who shout at one another in the streets, who whistle at the top of their lungs, or leave doors to slam in the faces of those behind them.

His resentment against these practices was made the more bitter by the knowledge that he was absolutely helpless in the matter whenever he came within hearing distance of an ill-bred person.

There was yet another element in this which added to his misery. He said to me once, when we had been driven off the plage at Mentone by two American tourists of the worst type, who at a hundred yards' distance from each other were yelling their views as to which hotel they proposed to meet at for lunch, "I can never forget that when I was a young man in the full vigor of my health I used to regard other people's complaints about noise as being merely an affectation. I would even make a noise deliberately in order to annoy any one who forced the absurd p retense upon my notice. Well, Mr. Ireland, I swear my punishment has been heavy enough."

To revert, however, to Mr. Pulitzer's dependence on those around him, it must be remembered that nothing could reach him except through the medium of speech. The state of his bank account, the condition of his investments, the reports about The World, his business correspondence, the daily news in which he was so deeply interested, everything upon which he based his relation with the affairs of life he had to accept at second hand.

It might be supposed that under these circumstances Mr.

Pulitzer was easily deceived, that when there was no evil intention, for instance, but simply a desire to spare him annoyance, the exercise of a little ingenuity could shield him from anything likely to wound his feelings or excite his anger. As a matter of fact I have never known a man upon whom it would not have been easier to practice a deception. His blindness, so far from being a hindrance to him in reaching the truth, was an aid.

Two instances will serve to illustrate the point. Suppose that I found in the morning paper an article which I thought would stir J. P. up and spoil his day: when I was called to read to him I had no means of knowing whether the man whom I replaced had taken the same view as myself and had skipped the article or whether he had, deliberately or inadvertently, read it to him. The same argument applied to the man who was to follow me. If I read the article to him I might find out later that my predecessor had omitted it, or, if I omitted it, that my successor had read it.

In either event one of us would be in the wrong; and it was impossible to tell in advance whether the man who read it would be blamed for lack of discretion or praised for his good judgment, as everything depended upon the exact mood in which Mr. Pulitzer happened to be.

It was an awkward dilemma for the secretary, for, if he did not read it and another man did, Mr. Pulitzer might very well interpret the first man's caution as an effort to hoodwink him, or the second man's boldness as an exhibition of indifference to his feelings, or, what was more likely still, fasten one fault upon one man and the other upon the other.

The same problem presented itself from a different direction. Often, Mr. Pulitzer would take out of his pocket a bundle of papers - newspaper clippings, letters, statistical reports, and memoranda of various kinds. Handing them to his companion he would say:

"Look through these and see if there is a letter with the London post mark, and a sheet of blue paper with some figures on it."

You could never tell what was behind these inquiries. Sometimes he was content to know that the papers were there, sometimes he asked you to read them, and as he might very well have them read to him by several people during the day he had a perfect check on all printed or written matter once it was in his hands.

In addition to all this his exquisite sense of hearing enabled him to detect the slightest variation in your tone of voice. If you hesitated or betrayed the least uneasiness his suspicions were at once aroused and he took steps to verify from other sources any statement you made under such circumstances.

It will be readily understood that with his keen and analytic mind Mr. Pulitzer very soon discovered exactly what kind of work was best suited to the capacities of each of his secretaries. Thus to Mr. Paterson was assigned the reading of history and biography, to Mr. Pollard, a Harvard man and the only American on the personal staff during my time, novels and plays in French and English, to Herr Mann German literature of all kinds. Thwaites was chiefly occupied with Mr. Pulitzer's correspondence, and Craven with the yacht accounts, though they, as well as myself, had roving commissions covering the periodical literature of France, Germany, England, and America.

This division of our reading was by no means rigid; it represented Mr. Pulitzer's view of our respective spheres of greatest utility; but it was often disturbed by one or another of us going on sick leave or falling a victim to the weather when we were at sea.

Subject to such chances Pollard always read to Mr. Pulitzer during his breakfast hour, and Mann during his siesta, while the reading after dinner was pretty evenly divided between

Pollard, Paterson, and myself.

If Mr. Pulitzer once got it into his head that a particular man was better than any one else for a particular class of work nothing could reconcile him to that man's absence when such work was to be done.

An amusing instance of this occurred on an occasion when Pollard was sea-sick and could not read to J. P. at breakfast. I was hurriedly summoned to take his place. I was dumb-founded, for I had never before been called upon for this task, and Mr. Pulitzer had often held it up to me as the last test of fitness, the charter of your graduation. I had nothing whatever prepared of the kind which J. P. required at that time, and I knew that upon the success of his breakfast might very well depend the general complexion of his whole day.

In desperation I rushed into Pollard's cabin, and its unhappy occupant, with a generosity which even seasickness could not chill, gave me a bundle of Spectators, Athenaeums, and Literary Digests, with pencil marks in the margins indicating exactly what he had intended to read in the ordinary course of things. I breathed a sigh of relief and hastened to the library, where I found J. P. very nervous and out of sorts after a bad night.

He immediately began to deplore Pollard's absence, on the ground that it was impossible for anyone to know what to read to him at breakfast without years of experience and training. I said nothing, feeling secure with Pollard's prepared "breakfast food," as we called it, in front of me. I awaited only his signal to begin reading, confident that I could win laurels for myself without robbing Pollard, whose wreath was firmly fixed on his brow.

Alas for my hopes! My very first sentence destroyed my chances, for I had the misfortune to begin reading something which he had already heard. Nothing annoyed him more than this; and we all made a habit of writing "Dead" across any

Alleyne Ireland

article in a periodical as soon as J. P. had had it, so that we could keep off each other's trails. I am willing to believe that this was the first and only time that Pollard ever forgot to kill an article after he had read it, but it was enough, in the deplorable state of Mr. Pulitzer's nerves that morning, to inflict a wound upon my reputation as a breakfast-time reader which months did not suffice to heal.

With such a bad start Mr. Pulitzer immediately concluded that I was useless, and he worked himself up into such a state about it that passage after passage, carefully marked by Pollard, was greeted with,

"Stop! Stop! For God's sake!" or,

"Next! Next!" or,

"My God! Is there much more of that?" or,

"Well, Mr. Ireland, isn't there ANYTHING interesting in all those papers?"

I bore up manfully against this until he made the one remark I could not stand.

"Now, Mr. Ireland," he said, his voice taking on a tone of gentle reproach, "I know you've done your best, but it is very bad. If you don't believe me, just take those papers to Mr. Pollard when he feels better; don't disturb him now when he's ill; and show him what you read to me. Now, just for fun, I'd like you to do that. He will tell you that there is not a single line which you have read that he would have read had he been in your place. I hope I haven't been too severe with you; but I hold up my hands and swear that Mr. Pollard wouldn't have read me a line of that rubbish."

This was too much! Carefully controlling my voice so that no trace of malice should be detected in it, I replied:

"I took these papers off Mr. Pollard's table a moment before I came to you, and the parts I have read are the parts he had marked, with the intention of reading them to you himself."

I thought I had J. P. cornered. It was before I learned that there was no such thing as cornering J. P.

Leaning toward me, and putting a hand on my shoulder, he said:

"Now, boy, don't be put out about this. I do believe, honestly, that you did your best; but you should not make excuses. When you are wrong, admit it, and try and benefit by my advice. You will find a very natural explanation of your mistake. Perhaps the passages Mr. Pollard marked were the ones he did NOT intend to read to me, or perhaps you took the wrong set of papers; some perfectly natural explanation I am sure."

That night at dinner, when I was still smarting under the sense of injustice born of my morning's experience, J. P. gave me an opening which I could not allow to pass unused.

Turning to me during a pause in the conversation, he asked:

"And what have YOU been doing this afternoon, Mr. Ireland?"

A happy inspiration flashed across my mind, and I replied:

"I've been making a rough draft of a play, sir."

"Well, my God! I didn't know you wrote plays."

"Very seldom, at any rate; but I had an idea this morning that I couldn't resist."

"What is it to be called?" inquired J. P.

"'The Importance of being Pollard,'" I answered, whereupon J. P. and everyone else at the table had a good laugh. They had all been through a breakfast with J. P. when Pollard was away, and could sympathize with my feelings.

Mr. Pulitzer was very sensible of the difficulties which lay in everybody's path at the times when lack of sleep or a prolonged attack of pain had made him excessively irritable; and when he had recovered from one of these periods of strain, and was conscious of having been rough in his manner, he often took occasion to make amends.

Sometimes he would do this when we were at table, adopting a humorous tone as he said, "I'm afraid so-and-so will never forgive me for the way I treated him this afternoon; but I want to say that he really read me an excellent story and read it very well, and that I am grateful to him. I was feeling wretchedly ill and had a frightful headache, and if I said anything that hurt his feelings I apologize."

Once, during my weeks of probation, when J. P. felt that he had carried his test of my good temper beyond reason, he stopped suddenly in our walk, laid a hand on my shoulder, and asked:

"What do you feel when I am unreasonable with you? Do you feel angry? Do you bear malice?"

"Not at all," I replied. "I suppose my feeling is very much like that of a nurse for a patient. I realize that you are suffering and that you are not to be held responsible for what you do at such times."

"I thank you for that, Mr. Ireland," he replied. "You never said anything which pleased me more. Never forget that I am blind, and that I am in pain most of the time."

A matter which I had reason to notice at a very early stage of my acquaintance with Mr. Pulitzer was that when he was in a bad mood it was the worst possible policy to offer no resistance to his pressure. It was part of his nature to go forward in any direction until he encountered an obstacle. When he reached one he paused before making up his mind whether he would go through it or round it. The further he went the more interested he became, his purpose always being to discover a boundary, whether of your knowledge, of your patience, of your memory, or of your nervous endurance.

He never respected a man who did not at some point stand up and resist him. After the line had once been drawn at that point, and his curiosity had been gratified, he was always careful not to approach it too closely; and it was only on the rare occasions when he was in exceptionally bad condition that any clash occurred after the first one had been settled.

I put off my own little fight for a long time, partly because I was very much affected by the sight of his wretchedness, and partly because I did not at first realize how necessary it was for him to find out just how far my self-control could be depended upon. As soon as this became clear to me I determined to seize the first favorable opportunity which presented itself of getting into my intrenchments and firing a blank cartridge or two.

It was after I had been with him about a month that my chance came. I had noticed that his manner toward me was slowly but steadily growing more hostile, and I had been expecting daily to receive my dismissal from the courteous hands of Dunningham, or to find myself unable to go further with the ordeal.

Finally, I consulted Dunningham, and was informed by him, to my great surprise, that I was doing very well and that Mr. Pulitzer was pleased with me. This information cleared the ground in front of me, and that afternoon when I was called to walk with Mr. Pulitzer I decided to put out a danger signal if I was hard pressed.

Everything favored such a course. J. P. had enjoyed a good siesta and was feeling unusually well; if, therefore, he was very disagreeable I would know that it was from design and not from an attack of nerves. Furthermore, he selected a subject of conversation in regard to which I was as well, if not better, informed than he was - a question relating to British Colonial policy.

The moment I began to speak I saw that his object was to drive me to the wall. He flatly contradicted me again and again, insinuated that I had never met certain statesmen whose words I repeated, and, finally, after I had concluded my arguments in support of the view I was advancing, he said in an angry tone, assumed for the occasion, of course:

"Mr. Ireland, I am really distressed that we should have had this discussion. I had hoped that, with years of training and advice, I might have been able to make something out of you; but any man who could seriously hold the opinion you have expressed, and could attempt to justify it with the mass of inaccuracies and absurdities that you have given me, is simply a damned fool."

"I am sorry you said that, Mr. Pulitzer," I replied in a very serious voice.

"Why, for God's sake, you don't mind my calling you a damned fool, do you?"

"Not in the least, sir. But when you call me a damned fool you shatter an ideal I held about you."

"What's that? An ideal about me? What do you mean?"

"Well, sir, years before I met you I had heard that if there was one thing above all others which distinguished you from all other journalists it was that you had the keenest nose for news of any man living."

"What has that to do with my calling you a damned fool?"

"Simply this, that the fact that I'm a damned fool hasn't been news to me any time during the past twenty years."

He saw the point at once, laughed heartily and, putting an arm round my shoulders, as was his habit with all of us when he wished to show a friendly feeling or take the edge off a severe rebuke, said:

"Now, boy, you're making fun of me, and you must not make fun of a poor old blind man. Now, then, I take it all back; I shouldn't have called you a damned fool."

It was from this moment that my relations with Mr. Pulitzer began to improve.

A few days after the incident which I have just related we dropped anchor in the Bay of Naples, and Mr. Pulitzer announced his intention of sailing for New York by a White Star boat the following afternoon. He asked me to go with him; and I accepted this invitation as the sign that my period of probation was over.

Everything was prepared for our departure. Dunningham worked indefatigably. He went aboard the White Star boat, arranged for the accommodation of our party, had partitions knocked down so that Mr. Pulitzer could have a private diningroom and a library, and convoyed aboard twenty or thirty trunks and cases containing books, mineral waters, wines, cigars, fruit, special articles of diet, clothes, fur coats, rugs, etc., for J. P.

We all packed our belongings, telegraphed to our friends, sent ashore for the latest issues of the magazines, and sat around in deck chairs waiting for the word to follow our things aboard the liner.

After half an hour of suspense Dunningham came out of the

Alleyne Ireland

library, where he had been in consultation with J. P., and as he advanced toward us we rose and made our way to the gangway, where one of the launches was swinging to her painter.

Dunningham, smiling and imperturbable as ever, raised his hand and said, "No, gentlemen, Mr. Pulitzer has changed his mind; we are not going to America. We remain on the yacht and sail this afternoon for Athens."

He disappeared over the side, and an hour or two later returned with the chef and the butler and one of the saloon stewards, who had gone aboard the liner to make things ready, and some tons of baggage.

We sailed just as the White Star boat cleared the end of the mole. When she passed us, within a hundred yards, she dipped her flag. I was walking with Mr. Pulitzer at the time and mentioned the exchange of salutes. He was silent for a few minutes. Then he asked, "Has she passed us?" "Yes," I replied, "she's half-a-mile ahead of us now." "Have you got your pad with you? Just make a note to ask Thwaites to cable to New York from the next port we call at and tell someone to send two hundred of the best Havana cigars to the captain. That man has some sense. Most captains would have blown their damned whistle when they dipped their flag. Have a note written to the captain telling him that I appreciated his consideration."

Our voyage to Athens and thence, through the Corinth Canal, back to Mentone, was free from incident. J. P. discussed the possibility of going to Constantinople or to Venice, but our cabled inquiries about the weather brought discouraging replies describing an unusually cold season, and these projects were abandoned.

About this time Mr. Pulitzer's health showed a marked improvement, which was reflected in the most agreeable manner in the general conditions of life on the yacht. He had been worried for some weeks about his plans for going to New

York, and this had interfered with his sleep, had increased his nervousness and aggravated every symptom of his physical weakness. With this matter finally disposed of he could look forward to a peaceful cruise, during which he would be able to catch up with his careful reading of the marked file of The World, and thus remove a weight from his mind.

He detested having work accumulate on his hands, but when his health was worse than usual this was unavoidable. He always drove himself to the last ounce of his endurance, and it was only when his condition indicated an imminent collapse that he would consent to drop everything except light reading, and to spend a few days out at sea without calling anywhere for letters, papers, or cables.

It was during this, our last, cruise in the Mediterranean that I discovered that Mr. Pulitzer was one of the best and most fascinating talkers I had ever heard. Once in a while, when he was feeling cheerful after a good night's rest and a pleasant day's reading, he monopolized the conversation at lunch or dinner. He was generally more willing to talk when we took our meals at a large round table on deck, for he loved the sea breeze and was soothed by it.

When he talked he simply compelled your attention. I often felt that, if he had not made his career otherwise, he might have been one of the world's greatest actors, or one of its most popular orators. In flexibility of tone, in variety of gesture, in the change of his facial expression he was the peer of anyone I have seen on the stage.

To an extraordinary flow of language he added a range of information and a vividness of expression truly astonishing. His favorite themes were politics and the lives of great men. To his monologues on the former subject he brought a ripe wisdom, based upon the most extensive reading and the shrewdest observation, and quickened by the keenest enthusiasm. He was by no means a political bigot; and there was not a political experiment, from the democracy of the Greeks to the referendum in Switzerland, with the details of which he was not perfectly familiar. Although he was a convinced believer in the Republican form of government, having, as he expressed it, "no use for the King business," he was fully alive to the peculiar dangers and difficulties with which modern progress has confronted popular institutions.

When the publication of some work like Rosebery's Chatham or Monypenny's Disraeli afforded an occasion, Mr. Pulitzer would spend an hour before we left the table in giving us a picture of some exciting crisis in English politics, the high lights picked out in pregnant phrases of characterization, in brilliant epitome of the facts, in spontaneous epigram, and illustrative anecdote. Whether he spoke of the Holland House circle, of the genius of Cromwell, of Napoleon's campaigns, or sought to point a moral from the lives of Bismarck, Metternich, Louis XI, or Kossuth, every sentence was marked by the same penetrating analysis, the same facility of expression, the same clearness of thought.

On rare occasions he talked of his early days, telling us in a charming, simple, and unaffected manner of the tragic and humorous episodes with which his youth had been crowded. Of the former I recall a striking description of a period during which he filled two positions in St. Louis, one involving eight hours' work during the day, the other eight hours during the night. Four of the remaining eight were devoted to studying English.

His first connection with journalism arose out of an experience which he related with a wealth of detail which showed how deeply it had been burned into his memory.

When he arrived in St. Louis he soon found himself at the end of his resources, and was faced with the absolute impossibility of securing work in that city. In company with forty other men he applied at the office of a general agent who had advertised for hands to go down the Mississippi and take up well-paid posts on a Louisiana sugar plantation. The agent demanded a fee of five dollars from each applicant, and, by pooling their resources, the members of this wretched band managed to meet the charge. The same night they were taken on board a steamer which immediately started down river. At three o'clock in the morning they were landed on the river bank about forty miles below St. Louis, at a spot where there was neither house, road, nor clearing. Before the marooned party had time to realize its plight the steamer had disappeared.

A council of war was held, and it was decided that they should tramp back to St. Louis, and put a summary termination to the agent's career by storming his office and murdering him. Whether or not this reckless program would have been carried out it is impossible to say, for when, three days later, the ragged army arrived in the city, worn out with fatigue and half dead from hunger, the agent had decamped.

A reporter happened to pick up the story, and by mere chance met Pulitzer and induced him to write out in German the tale of his experiences. This account created such an impression on the mind of the editor through whose hands it passed that Pulitzer was offered, and accepted, with the greatest misgivings, as he solemnly assured us, a position as reporter on the Westliche Post.

The event proved that there had been no grounds for J. P.'s modest doubts. After he had been some time on the paper, things went so badly that two reporters had to be got rid of. The editor kept Pulitzer on the staff, because he felt that if anyone was destined to force him out of the editorial chair it was not a young, uneducated foreigner, who could hardly mumble half-a-dozen words of English. The editor was mistaken. Within a few years J. P. not only supplanted him but became half-proprietor of the paper.

Another interesting anecdote of his early days, which he told with great relish, related to his experience as a fireman on a Mississippi ferryboat. His limited knowledge of English was regarded by the captain as a personal affront, and that fire-eating old-timer made it his particular business to let young Pulitzer feel the weight of his authority. At last the overwork and the constant bullying drove J. P. into revolt, and he left the boat after a violent quarrel with the captain.

Whenever J. P. reached this point in the story, and I heard him tell it several times, his face lighted up with amusement, and he had to stop until he had enjoyed a good laugh.

"Well, my God!" he would conclude, "about two years later, when I had learned English and studied some law and been made a notary public, this very same captain walked into my office in St. Louis one day to have some documents sealed. As soon as he saw me he stopped short, as if he had seen a ghost, and said, "Say, ain't you the damned cuss that I fired off my boat?"

"I told him yes, I was. He was the most surprised man I ever saw, but after he had sworn himself hoarse he faced the facts and gave me his business."

Mr. Pulitzer always declared that the proudest day of his life, the occasion on which his vanity was most tickled, was when he was elected to the Missouri Legislature. Things were evidently run in a rather happy-go-lucky fashion in those early days, since, as he admitted with a reminiscent smile, he was absolutely disqualified for election, being neither an American citizen nor of age.

Mr. Pulitzer's anecdotes about himself always ended in one way. He would break off suddenly and exclaim, "For Heaven's sake, why do you let me run on like this; as soon as a man gets into the habit of talking about his past adventures he might just as well make up his mind that he is growing old and that his intellect is giving way."

It was this strong disinclination for personal reminiscence which prevented Mr. Pulitzer, despite many urgent appeals, from writing his autobiography. It is a thousand pities that he adhered to this resolution, for his career, as well in point of interest as in achievement and picturesqueness, would have stood the test of comparison with that of any man whose life-story has been preserved in literature.

CHAPTER VI

WIESBADEN AND AN ATLANTIC VOYAGE

At last the time came when we had to leave the yacht and make a pilgrimage to Wiesbaden, in order that Mr. Pulitzer might submit to a cure before sailing for New York.

The first stage of our journey took us from Genoa to Milan. Here we stayed for five hours so that J. P. could have his lunch and his siesta comfortably at an hotel. Paterson had been sent ahead two or three days in advance to look over the hotels and to select the one which promised to be least noisy. On our arrival in Milan J. P. was taken to an automobile, and in ten minutes he was in his rooms.

Simple as these arrangements appear from the bald statement of what actually happened they really involved a great deal of care and forethought. It was not enough that Paterson should visit half-a-dozen hotels and make his choice from a cursory inspection. After his choice had been narrowed down by a process of elimination he had to spend several hours in each of two or three hotels, in the room intended for J. P., so that he could detect any of the hundred noises which might make the room uninhabitable to its prospective tenant.

The room might be too near the elevator, it might be too near a servants' staircase, it might overlook a courtyard where carpets were beaten, or a street with heavy traffic, it might be within earshot of a dining-room where an orchestra played or a smoking-room with the possibility of loud talking, it might open off a passage which gave access to some much frequented reception-room.

Most of these points could be determined by merely observing the location of the room. But other things were to be considered. Did the windows rattle, did the floor creak, did the doors open and shut quietly, was the ventilation good, were there noisy guests in the adjoining rooms?

This last difficulty was, I understand, usually overcome by Mr. Pulitzer engaging, in addition to his own room, a room on either side of it, three rooms facing it, the room above it and the room beneath it.

Even the question of the drive from the station to the hotel had to be thought out. A trial trip was made in an automobile. If the route followed a car line or passed any spot likely to be noisy, such as a market place or a school playground, or if it led over a roughly paved road on which the car would jolt, another route had to be selected, which, as far as possible, dodged the unfavorable conditions.

Our carefully arranged journey passed without incident. We had a private car from Milan to Frankfort and another for the short run to Wiesbaden, where we arrived in time for lunch on the day after our departure from Genoa. Everything had been prepared for our reception by some one who had made similar arrangements on former occasions. We occupied the whole of a villa belonging to one of the large hotels, and situated less than a hundred yards from it.

In the main our life was modeled upon that at the Cap Martin villa; but part of Mr. Pulitzer's morning was devoted to baths, massage, and the drinking of waters. Our meals were taken, as a rule, either in a private dining-room at the hotel or in the big restaurant of the Kurhaus; but when Mr. Pulitzer was feeling more than usually tired the table was laid in the dining-room of the villa.

Our dinners at the Kurhaus were a welcome change from our ordinary meals with their set routine of literary discussions. Mr. Pulitzer was immensely interested in people; but it was impossible for him to meet them, except on rare occasions, because the excitement was bad for his health. Whenever he dined in a crowded restaurant, however, our time was fully occupied in describing with the utmost minuteness the men, women, and children around us.

The Kurhaus was an excellent place for the exercise of our descriptive powers. In addition to the ordinary crowd of pleasure-seekers and health-hunters there were, during a great part of our visit, a large number of military men, for the Kaiser spent a week at Wiesbaden that year and reviewed some troops, and this involved careful preparation in advance by a host of court officials and high army officers.

Under these circumstances the dining-room of the Kurhaus presented a scene full of color and animation. Sometimes J. P. said to one of us: "Look around for a few minutes and pick out the most interesting-looking man and woman in the room, examine them carefully, try and catch the tone of their voices, and when you are ready describe them to me." Or he might say: "I hear a curious, sharp, incisive voice somewhere over there on my right. There it is now - don't you hear it? - s s s s, every s like a hiss. Describe that man to me; tell me what kind of people he's talking to; tell me what you think his profession is." Or it might be: "There are some gabbling women over there. Describe them to me. How are they dressed, are they painted, are they wearing jewels, how old are they?"

In whatever form the request was made its fulfilment meant a description covering everything which could be detected by the eye or surmised from any available clew.

Describing people to J. P. was by no means an easy task. It was no use saying that a man had a medium-sized nose, that he was of average height, and that his hair was rather dark. Everything had to be given in feet and inches and in definite colors. You had to exercise your utmost powers to describe the exact cast of the features, the peculiar texture and growth of the hair, the expression of the eyes, and every little trick of gait or gesture.

Mr. Pulitzer was very sceptical of everybody's faculty of description. He made us describe people, and specially his own children and others whom he knew well, again and again, and his unwillingness to accept any description as being good rested no doubt upon the wide divergence between the different descriptions he received of the same person.

There were few things which Mr. Pulitzer enjoyed more than having a face described to him, whether of a living person or of a portrait, and as our table-talk was often about men and women of distinction or notoriety, dead or living, any one of us might be called upon at any time to portray feature by feature some person whose name had been mentioned.

By providing ourselves with illustrated catalogues of the Royal Academy exhibitions and of the National Portrait Gallery, and by cutting out the portraits with which the modern publisher so lavishly decorates his announcements, we generally managed, by pulling together, to cover the ground pretty well. I have sat through a meal during which one or another of us furnished a microscopic description of the faces of Warren Hastings, Lord Clive, President Wilson, the present King and Queen of England, the late John W. Gates, Ignace Paderewski, and an odd dozen current murderers, embezzlers, divorce habitues, and candidates for political office.

The delicate enjoyment of this game was not reached, however, until, at the following meal, one of us, who had been absent at the original delineation, was asked to cover some of the ground that had been gone over a few hours earlier. Mr. Pulitzer would say: "Is Mr. So-and-So here? Well, now, just for fun, let us see what he has to say about the appearance of some of the people we spoke about at lunch."

The result was almost always an astonishing disclosure of the inability of intelligent people to observe closely, to describe accurately, and to reach any agreement as to the significance of what they have seen. It was bad enough when the latest witness had before him the actual pictures on which the first description had been based; even then crooked noses became straight, large mouths small, disdain was turned to affability and ingenuousness to guile; but where this guide was lacking the descriptions were often ludicrously discrepant.

While we were at Wiesbaden we seldom spent much time at the dinner table, as J. P. usually took his choice between walking in the garden of the Kurhaus and listening to the orchestra and going to the opera. One night we motored over to Frankfort to hear Der Rosenkavalier, but the excursion was a dismal failure. We had to go over a stretch of very bad road, and with J. P. shaken into a state of extreme nervousness the very modern strains of the opera failed to please.

At the end of the second act J. P., who had been growing more and more dismal as the music bumped along its disjointed course, either in vain search or in careful avoidance of anything resembling a pleasant sound, turned to me and said: "My God! I can't stand any more of this. Will you please go and find the automobile and bring it round to the main entrance. I want to go home."

I saw a great deal of Mr. Pulitzer while we were at Wiesbaden, owing to the circumstance that Paterson was called to England on urgent private affairs and Pollard was away on leave. The absence of these two men was as much regretted by the staff as it was by J. P. himself. Paterson was, from his extraordinary erudition, seldom at a loss for a topic of conversation which would rivet J. P.'s attention, and Pollard, who had been a number of years with J. P., was not only, on his own subjects, the conversational peer of Paterson, but was in addition, from his soothing voice and manner and from his long and careful study of J. P., invaluable as a mental and nervous sedative.

It was at Wiesbaden that I first began to read books regularly to J. P. I read him portions of the biographies of Parnell, of Sir William Howard Russell, of President Polk (very little of this), of Napoleon, of Martin Luther, and at least a third of Macaulay's Essays.

He was a great admirer of Lord Macaulay's writings and read them constantly, as he found in them most of the qualities which he admired - great descriptive power, political acumen, satire, neatness of phrase, apt comparisons and analogies, and shrewd analysis of character. Many passages he made me read over and over again at different times. I reproduce a few of his favorite paragraphs for the purpose of showing what appealed to his taste.

From the Essay on Sir William Temple, the following lines referring to the Right Hon. Thomas Peregrine Courtenay, who, after his retirement from public life, wrote the Memoirs of Temple and stated in his preface that experience had taught him the superiority of literature to politics for developing the kindlier feelings and conducing to an agreeable life:

He has little reason, in our opinion, to envy any of those who are still engaged in a pursuit from which, at most, they can only expect that, by relinquishing liberal studies and social pleasures, by passing nights without sleep and summers without one glimpse of the beauty of nature, they may attain that laborious, that invidious, that closely watched slavery which is mocked with the name of power.

More often than any others I read him the following passages from the Essay on Milton:

The final and permanent fruits of liberty are wisdom, moderation, and mercy. Its immediate effects are often atrocious crimes, conflicting errors, scepticism on points the most clear, dogmatism on points the most mysterious. It is just at this crisis that its enemies love to exhibit it. They pull down the scaffolding from the half-finished edifice: they point to the flying dust, the falling bricks, the comfortless rooms, the frightful irregularity of the whole appearance; and then ask in scorn where the promised splendor and comfort is to be found. If such miserable sophisms were to prevail there would never be a good house or a good government in the world.

There is only one cure for the evils which newly acquired freedom produces; and that cure is freedom.

The blaze of truth and liberty may at first dazzle and bewilder nations which have become half blind in the house of bondage. But let them gaze on, and they will soon be able to bear it. In a few years men learn to reason. The extreme violence of opinion subsides. Hostile theories correct each other. The scattered elements of truth cease to contend, and begin to coalesce. And at length a system of justice and order is educed out of the chaos.

If men are to wait for liberty till they become wise and good in slavery, they may indeed wait forever.

I was surprised one day on returning to the villa after a walk in the Kurhaus gardens with J. P. to find an addition to our company in the person of the second gentleman who had examined me in London at the time I had applied for the post of secretary to Mr. Pulitzer.

This gentleman occupied what I imagine must have been the only post of its kind in the world. He was, in addition to whatever other duties he performed, Mr. Pulitzer's villa-seeker.

It was Mr. Pulitzer's custom to talk a good deal about his future plans, not those for the immediate future, in regard to which he was usually very reticent, but those for the following year, or for a vague "someday" when many things were to be done which as yet were nothing more than the toys with which his imagination delighted to play.

As he always spent a great part of the year in Europe, a

residence had to be found for him, it might be in Vienna, or London, or Berlin, or Mentone, or in any other place which emerged as a possibility out of the long discussions of the next year's itinerary.

Whenever the arguments in favor of any place had so far prevailed that a visit there had been accepted in principle as one of our future movements it became the duty of the villa-seeker to go to the locality, to gather a mass of information about its climate, its amenities, its resident and floating population, its accessibility by sea and land, the opportunities for hearing good music, and to report in the minutest detail upon all available houses which appeared likely to suit Mr. Pulitzer's needs.

These reports were accompanied by maps, plans, and photo-graphs, and they were considered by J. P. with the utmost care. Particular attention was paid to the streets and to the country roads in the neighborhood, as it was necessary to have facilities for motoring, for riding, and for walking.

The next step was to secure a villa, and after that had been done the alterations had to be undertaken which would make it habitable for J. P. These might be of a comparatively simple nature, a matter of fitting silencers to the doors and putting up double windows to keep out the noise; but they might extend much further and involve more or less elaborate changes in the interior arrangements. Even after all this had been done a sudden shift of plans might send the villa-seeker scurrying across Europe to begin the whole process over again in order to be prepared for new developments.

At the time I left London to join J. P. at Mentone I had stipulated that, if I should chance to be selected to fill the vacant post, I should not be called upon to take up my duties until I had returned to London and spent a fortnight there in clearing up my private affairs.

After we had been a few weeks at Wiesbaden it became

absolutely necessary for me to go to London for that purpose; and this led to a struggle with J. P. which nearly brought our relations to an end.

As soon as I broached the subject of a fortnight's leave of absence J. P. set his face firmly against the proposal. This was due not so much to any feeling on his part that my absence would be an inconvenience to him, for both Paterson and Pollard had returned to duty, but to an almost unconquerable repugnance he had to any one except himself initiating any plan which would in the slightest degree affect his arrangements. His sensitiveness on this point was so delicate that it was impossible, for instance, for any of us to accept an invitation to lunch or dine with friends who might happen to be in our neighborhood, or to ask for half a day off for any purpose whatever.

I do not mean to say that we never got away for a meal or that we were never free for a few hours; as a matter of fact, J. P. was by no means ungenerous in such things once a man had passed the trial stage; but, although J. P. might say to you, "Take two days off and amuse yourself," or "Take the evening off, and don't trouble to get back to work until lunch-time to-morrow," it was out of the question for you to say to J. P.: "An old friend of mine is here for the day, would you mind my taking lunch with him?"

No one, I am sure, ever made a suggestion of that kind to J. P. more than once - the effect upon him was too startling.

J. P.'s favors in the way of giving time off were always granted subject to a change of mind on his part; and these changes were often so sudden that it was our custom as soon as leave was given to disappear from the yacht or the villa at the earliest possible moment. But at times even an instant departure was too slow, for it might happen that before you were out of the room J. P. would say: "Just a moment, Mr. So-and-So, you wouldn't mind if I asked you to put off your holiday till to-morrow, would you? I think I would like you to finish that novel this evening; I am really interested to see how it comes out."

This, of course, was rather disappointing; but the great disadvantage of not getting away was that Mr. Pulitzer's memory generally clung very tenaciously to the fact that he had given you leave, and lost the subsequent act of rescinding it. The effect of this was that for the practical purpose of getting a day off your turn was used up as soon as J. P. granted it, without any reference to whether you actually got it or not; and the phrase, "until to-morrow," was not to be interpreted literally or to be acted upon without a further distinct permission.

The only "right" any of us had to time off was to our annual vacation of two weeks, which we had to take whenever J. P. wished. If, for any reason, one of us wanted leave of absence for a week or so, the matter had to be put into the hands of the discreet and diplomatic Dunningham; and so when the time came when I simply had to go to London it was to Dunningham I went for counsel.

Judging by the results, his intercession on my behalf was not very successful, for, on the occasion of our next meeting, J. P. made it clear to me that if I insisted on going to London it would be on pain of his displeasure and at the peril of my post. As I look back upon the incident, however, it is quite clear to me that the whole of his arguments and his dark hints were launched merely to test my sense of duty to those persons in London whom I had promised to see.

A day or two later J. P. told me that as I was going to London I might as well stay there for a month or two before joining him in New York. He outlined a course of study for me, which included lessons in speaking (my voice being harsh and unpleasant) and visits to all the principal art galleries, theaters and other places of interest, with a view to describing everything when I rejoined him.

On the eve of my departure Dunningham handed me, with Mr. Pulitzer's compliments, an envelope containing a handsome present, in the most acceptable form a present can take.

It was not until I was in the train, and the train had started, that I was able to realize that I was free. During the journey to London my extraordinary experiences of the past three months detached themselves from the sum of my existence and became cloaked with that haze of unreality which belongs to desperate illness or to a tragedy looked back upon from days of health and peace. Walking down St. James's Street twenty-four hours after leaving Wiesbaden, J. P. and the yacht and the secretaries invaded my memory not as things experienced but as things seen in a play or read in a story long ago.

I lost no time in making myself comfortable in London. Inquiries directed to the proper quarter soon brought me into touch with a gentleman to whose skill, I was assured, no voice, however disagreeable, could fail to respond. I saw my friends, my business associates, my tailor. I went to see Fanny's First Play three times, the National Portrait Gallery twice, the National Gallery once, and laid out my plans to see all the places in London (shame forbidding me to enumerate them) which every Englishman ought to have seen and which I had not seen.

This lasted for about two weeks, during which I saw something of Craven, who had left us in Naples to study something or other in London, and who was under orders to hold himself in readiness to go to New York with J. P. We dined at my club one night, and when I returned to my flat I found a telegram from Mr. Tuohy, instructing me to join J. P. in Liverpool the next day in time to sail early in the afternoon on the Cedric, as it had been decided to leave Craven in London for the present.

The voyage differed but little from our cruises in the yacht. J. P. took his meals in his own suite, and as Mrs. Pulitzer and Miss Pulitzer were on board they usually dined with him, one of the secretaries making a fourth at table.

In the matter of guarding J. P. from noise, extraordinary precautions were taken. Heavy mats were laid outside his cabin, specially made a dozen years before and stored by the White Star people waiting his call; that portion of the deck which surrounded his suite was roped off so that the passengers could not promenade there; and a close-fitting green baize door shut off the corridor leading to his quarters. His meals were served by his own butler and by one of the yacht stewards; and his daily routine went on as usual.

During the voyage I was broken in to the task of reading the magazines to J. P. So far as current issues were concerned I had to take the ones he liked best - The Atlantic Monthly, The American Magazine, The Quarterly Review, The Edinburgh Review, The World's Work, and The North American Review - and thoroughly master their contents.

While I was engaged on this sufficiently arduous labor I made, on cards, lists of the titles of all the articles and abstracts of all the more important ones. I have by me as I write a number of these lists, and I reproduce one of them.

The following list of articles represents what Mr. Pulitzer got from me in a highly condensed form during ONE HOUR: "The Alleged Passing of Wagner," "The Decline and Fall of Wagner," "The Mission of Richard Wagner," "The Swiftness of Justice in England and in the United States," "The Public Lands of the United States," "New Zealand and the Woman's Vote," "The Lawyer and the Community," "The Tariff Make-believe," "The Smithsonian Institute," "The Spirit and Letter of Exclusion," "The Panama Canal and American Shipping," "The Authors and Signers of the Declaration of Independence," "The German Social Democracy," "The Changing Position of American Trade," "The Passing of Polygamy."

I remember very well the occasion on which I gave him these articles. We were walking on one of the lower promenade decks of the Cedric, and J. P. asked me if I had any magazine articles ready for him. I told him, having the list of articles in my left hand, that I had fifteen ready. He pulled out his watch, and holding it toward me said:

"What time is it?"

"Twelve o'clock," I replied.

"Very good; that gives us an hour before lunch. Now go on with your articles; I'll allow you four minutes for each of them."

He did not actually take four minutes for each, for some of them did not interest him after my summary had run for a minute or so, but we just got the fifteen in during the hour.

After all that was possible had been done in the way of reducing the number of magazine articles, by rejecting the unsuitable ones, and their length by careful condensation, we were unable to keep pace with the supply. When a hundred or so magazines had accumulated Mr. Pulitzer had the lists of contents read to him, and from these he selected the articles which he wished to have read; and these arrears were disposed of when an opportunity presented itself.

At times Mr. Pulitzer did not feel well enough to take this concentrated mental food, and turned for relief to novels, plays and light literature; at times, when he was feeling unusually well, he occupied himself for several days in succession with matters concerning The World - in dictating editorials, letters of criticism, instruction and inquiry, or in considering the endless problems relating to policy, business management, personnel, and the soaring price of white paper.

An interesting feature of his activity on behalf of The World was his selection of new writers. Although his supervision of the paper extended to every branch, from advertising to news, from circulation to color-printing, it was upon the editorial page that he concentrated his best energies and his keenest observation.

It is no exaggeration to say that the editorial page of The World was to J. P. what a child is to a parent. He had watched it daily for a quarter of a century. During that time, I am told, he had read to him seventy-five per cent. of all the editorials which were printed on it, and had every cartoon described. Those who are interested in the editorial page of The World should read Mr. John L. Heaton's admirable History of a Page, published last year.

J. P.'s theory of editorial writing, which I heard him propound a dozen times, called for three cardinal qualities - brevity, directness and style - and, as these could not be expected to adorn hasty writing, he employed a large staff of editorial writers and tried to limit each man to an average of half a column a day, unless exceptional circumstances called for a lengthy treatment of some important question.

He watched the style of each man with the closest attention, examining the length of the paragraphs, of the sentences, of the words, the variety of the vocabulary, the choice of adjectives and adverbs, the employment of superlatives, the selection of a heading, the nicety of adjustment between the thought to be expressed and the language employed for its expression.

If he chanced in the course of his reading to run across any apt phrase in regard to literary style he would get one of us to type a number of copies and send one to each of the editorial writers on The World. The following were sent from Wiesbaden:

"Thiers compares a perfect style to glass through which we look without being conscious of its presence between the object and the eye." (From Abraham Hayward's "Essay on Thiers.")

"Lessing, Lichtenberger, and Schopenhauer agreed in saying that it is difficult to write well, that no man naturally writes well, and that one must, in order to acquire a style, work STRENUOUSLY ... I have tried to write well."(Nietzsche.)

J. P. was never tired of discussing literary style, of making comparisons between one language and another from the point of view of an exact expression of an idea, or of the different SOUND of the same idea expressed in different languages. For instance, he asked us once during an argument about translations of Shakespeare to compare the lines:

"You are my true and honorable wife,
As dear to me as are the ruddy drops
That visit my sad heart."

with the German:

"Ihr seid mein echtes, ehrenwertes Weib,
So teuer mir, als wie die Purpurtropfen
Die um mein trauernd Herz sich drangen."

and the opening words of Hamlet's soliloquy with the German:

"Sein oder Nichtsein, das ist hier die Frage."

Of the former pair he greatly preferred the English, of the latter the German.

Sometimes we discussed at great length the exact English equivalent of some German or French word. I remember one which he came back to again and again, the word leichtsinnig. We suggested as translations, frivolous, irresponsible, hare-brained, thoughtless, chicken-witted, foolish, crazy; but we never found an expression which suited him.

But I have wandered away from the subject of editorial writers. During the time I was with J. P. he selected two, and his method of selection is of interest in view of the great importance he attached to the editorial page of The World.

As I have said elsewhere, J. P. got practically all the important articles from every paper of consequence in the United States. If he read an editorial which impressed him, possibly from a Chicago or a San Francisco paper, he put it on one side and told Pollard, who read all this kind of material to him, to watch the clippings from that paper and to pick out any other editorials which he could identify as the work of the same man. Five years with J. P. had made Pollard an expert in penetrating the disguise of the editorial "We."

As soon as a representative collection of the unknown man's writings had been made J. P. instructed some one on The World to find out who the author was and to request that he would supply what he considered to be a fair sample of his work, a dozen or more articles, and a brief biography of himself.

If Mr. Pulitzer was satisfied with these an offer would be made to the man to join the staff of The World. Sometimes even these gentlemen were summoned to New York, to Bar Harbor, to Wiesbaden, or to Mentone, according to circumstances. I have met several of them, and they all agree in saying that the hardest work they ever did in their lives was to keep pace with Mr. Pulitzer while they were running the gauntlet of his judgment.

There are few men highly placed on The World to-day who have not been through such an ordeal. I doubt if any man was ever served by a staff whose individual ability, temper, resources and limitations were so minutely known to their employer. He knew them to the last ounce of their endurance, to the last word of their knowledge, beyond the last veil which enables even the most intelligent man to harbor, mercifully, a few delusions about himself.

To those who did not know Mr. Pulitzer it may appear that I

exaggerate his powers in this direction. As a matter of fact I believe that it would be impossible to do so.

When he had his sight he judged men as others judge them, and, making full allowance for his genius for observation and analysis, he was no doubt influenced to some extent by appearance, manners and associations. But after he became blind and retired from contact with all men, except a circle which cannot have exceeded a score in number, his judgment took on a new measure of clearness and perspective.

As a natural weapon of self-defense he developed a system of searching examination before which no subterfuge could stand. It was minute, persistent, comprehensive and ingenious in the last degree. It might begin to-day, reach an apparent conclusion, and be renewed after a month's silence. In the meantime, while the whole matter was becoming dim in your mind, inquiries had been made in a dozen directions in regard to the points at issue; and when the subject was reopened you were confronted not only with J. P.'s perfect memory of what you had said but with a detailed knowledge of matters which you had passed by as unimportant, or deliberately avoided for any one of a dozen perfectly honest reasons.

J. P.'s questions covered names, places, dates, motives, the chain of causation, what you said, what you did, what you felt, what you thought, the reasons why you felt, thought, acted as you did, the reasons why your thought and action had not been such-and-such, your opinion of your own conduct, in looking back upon the episode, your opinion of the thoughts, actions and feelings of everybody else concerned, your conjectures as to THEIR motives, what you would do if you were again faced with the same problem, why you would do it, why you had not done it on the previous occasion.

Starting at any point in your career Mr. Pulitzer worked backward and forward until all that you had ever thought or done, from your earliest recollection down to the present moment, had been disclosed to him so far as he was interested to know it, and your memory served you.

This process varied in length according to the nature of the experiences of the person subjected to it, and to the precise quality of Mr. Pulitzer's interest in him. In my own case it lasted about three months and was copiously interspersed with written statements by myself of facts about myself, opinions by myself about myself, and endless references to people I had known during the past twenty-five years.

Mr. Pulitzer's attitude toward references was the product of vast experience. He complained that scores of men had come to him with references from some of the most distinguished people living, references so glowing that one man should have been ashamed to write them and the other ashamed to receive them, references of such a character that their happy possessors might, without being guilty of immodesty, have applied for the Chief Justiceship of the United States, the Viceroyalty of India, the Archbishopric of Canterbury, the Presidency of the Royal College of Surgeons, or the Mastership of Baliol, but that the great majority of these men had turned out to be ignorant, lazy and stupid to an unbelievable degree.

When the question of my own references came up I begged in a humorous way that, having heard J. P.'s views about the value of testimonials, my friends should be spared the useless task of eulogizing me.

"No, my God!" exclaimed J. P. "None of them shall be spared. What I said about testimonials is all perfectly true; but it only serves to show what sort of person a man must be who can't even get testimonials. No, no; if a man brings references it proves nothing; but if he can't, it proves a great deal."

Our voyage to New York was marred by but one distressing feature, the behavior of two infants, one of whom cried all day and the other all night. J. P. stood it very well. I think he regarded it as one of the few necessary noises. He suffered from it, of course, but the only remark he ever made to me about it was:

"I really think that one of the most extraordinary things in the world is the amount of noise a child can make. Here we are with a sixty-mile gale blowing and some ten thousand horse-power engines working inside the ship, and yet that child can make itself heard from one end of the boat to the other. I think there must be two of them; the sound is not quite the same at night. Now, Mr. Ireland, do, just for the fun of it, find out about that. Don't let the mother know - I wouldn't like to hurt her feelings; but ask one of the stewards about it."

In due course we reached New York. The Liberty, which had crossed directly from Marseilles, met us at quarantine, and Mr. Pulitzer was transferred to her without landing. The rest of us joined the yacht the same evening. That night we sailed for Bar Harbor.

CHAPTER VII

BAR HARBOR AND THE LAST CRUISE

During the forenoon of the following day we dropped anchor opposite the water-front of Mr. Pulitzer's Bar Harbor estate. The house was situated right on the rocky foreshore, and was backed by extensive grounds which completely cut it off from the noise of the traffic on the main road.

By means of a flight of granite steps, leading down from a lawn laid along the whole of the house-front, within containing walls, access was had to a pier to the end of which was attached a floating pontoon affording an easy means of boarding the yacht's boats or the launches which were kept at Chatwold for use when the house was occupied.

Chatwold was a big, rambling place, which had been added to from time to time until it was capable of accommodating about twenty people in addition to J. P., whose quarters were in a large granite structure, specially designed with a view to securing complete quietness. This building was in the form of a tower about forty feet square and four stories high. On the ground floor was a magnificent room, occupying the whole length of the tower and two-thirds of its breadth, which served as a library and dining-room for J. P. On the side facing the sea there was a large verandah where Mr. Pulitzer took his breakfast and where he sat a great deal during the day when he was transacting business or being read to.

The whole of the basement of the tower was taken up by a swimming pool and dressing rooms. The water was pumped in from the sea and could be heated by a system of steam pipes. The upper floors of the tower were given over to bedrooms, for J. P., for the major-domo and for several of the secretaries.

Most of the servants were housed in a large building some distance from the main residence, and there were separate quarters for the grooms and stablemen, and for the heard gardener and his assistants.

While we were at Chatwold there was a gathering of the Pulitzer family - Mrs. Joseph Pulitzer, a cousin of Jefferson Davis and a belle of Washington in her day, who married Mr. Pulitzer years before his success in life had been made and when the fight for his place in journalism was still in its early stages; Mr. and Mrs. Ralph Pulitzer and their young son, Ralph; Mr. and Mrs. Joseph Pulitzer, Jr., Miss Edith Pulitzer, Miss Constance Pulitzer and Mr. Pulitzer's youngest child, Herbert, a boy of fifteen.

The presence of the family had little effect upon the routine of Mr. Pulitzer's daily life. He saw as much of his wife and children as he could; but the intensity of his family emotions was such that they could only be given rein at the price of sleepless nights, savage pain, and desperate weariness. His interest in everything concerning the family was overwhelming, his curiosity inexhaustible. Everybody had to be described over and over again, but especially young Master Ralph, a bright and handsome child, born long after his grandfather had become totally blind, and Master Herbert, of whose appearance he retained only a memory of the dim impressions he had been able to gather years before when a little sight yet remained to him.

It was at lunch and at dinner that Mr. Pulitzer saw most of the family. He almost always took his meals in the library at a table seating four; and the party usually included Mrs. Pulitzer, one of the other ladies or Master Herbert, and a secretary. I was present at a great many of these gatherings, partly because J. P. had gradually acquired a taste for such humor as I was able to contribute to the conversation, and partly because he relished a salad-dressing which represented my only accomplishment in the gastronomic field.

A feature of the Bar Harbor life which Mr. Pulitzer enjoyed greatly and which he could not indulge in elsewhere were the long trips he made in a big electric launch on the sheltered waters of Frenchman's Bay. When the weather was fine these trips occupied two or three hours each day. J. P. sat in an armchair amidships, with two companions, very often his two older sons, to read to him or to discuss business affairs.

On the occasions when I formed one of the party I had the opportunity of observing that so far as the quantity and the quality of work were concerned it was an easier task to be one of Mr. Pulitzer's secretaries than to be one of his sons. I have never seen men put to a more severe test of industry, concentration, and memory than were Mr. Ralph and Mr. Joseph, Jr., while they were at Bar Harbor or on the yacht.

It is a pleasure to bear witness to the affectionate solicitude, the patience, and the good will with which they met the exacting demands of their father. They realized, of course, as every one who worked for J. P. realized it, that the weight of the burden he placed upon you and the strictness of the account to which you were called were the truest measure of his regard.

Next to politics there was nothing which interested J. P. more than molding and developing the people around him; and what was no more than a strong interest when it concerned his employees became a passion when it concerned his sons. His activities in this direction ministered alike to his love of power and to his horror of wasted talents; they gratified his ever-present desire to discover the boundaries of human character and intellect, to explore the mazes of human temperament and emotion.

What you knew and what you were able to do, once you had reached a certain standard, became secondary in his interest to what you could be made to know and what you could be taught to do. He was never content that a man should stand upon his record; growth and development were the chief aims of his discipline.

His method was well illustrated in my own case. One of his earliest injunctions to me was that I should never introduce any subject of conversation connected, in however remote a degree, with my travels or with my studies in relation to the government of tropical dependencies. When, for instance, he happened to need some information about India or the West Indies, he always directed one of the other men to find it for him. This arrangement had, from his standpoint, the double advantage of making the other man learn something of which he was ignorant, and of leaving me free to work at something of which I was ignorant. Thus J. P. killed two intellectual birds with one stone.

It was not only in regard to mental accomplishments, however, that J. P. pursued his plan of educating everybody around him. He insisted, among other things, that I should learn to ride, not because there was any lack of people who could ride with him, but because by means of application I could add a new item to the list of things I could do. After a dozen lessons from a groom I progressed so far that, having acquired the ability to stay more or less in the saddle while the horse trotted, Mr. Pulitzer frequently took me riding with him.

We always rode three abreast - a groom on J. P.'s right and myself on his left; and conversation had to be kept up the whole time. This presented no peculiar difficulties when the horses were walking, but when they trotted I found it no easy task to keep my seat, to preserve the precise distance from J. P. which saved me from touching his stirrup and yet allowed me to speak without raising my voice, and to leave enough of my mind unoccupied to remember my material and to present it without betraying the discomfort of my position.

During these rides, and especially when we were walking our horses along a quiet, shady stretch of road, J. P. sometimes became reminiscent. On one of these occasions he told me the story of how he lost his sight. As I wrote it down as soon as we got back to the house, I can tell it almost in his own words.

We had been discussing the possibility of his writing an autobiography, and he said, throwing his head back and smiling reflectively:

"Well, I sometimes wish it could be done. It would make an interesting book; but I do not think I shall ever do it. My God! I work from morning to night as it is. When would I get the time?" Then suddenly changing his mood: "It won't do any harm for you to make a few notes now and then, and some day, perhaps, we might go through them and see if there is anything worth preserving. Has any one ever told you how I lost my sight? No? Well, it was in November, 1887. The World had been conducting a vigorous campaign against municipal corruption in New York - a campaign which ended in the arrest of a financier who had bought the votes of aldermen in order to get a street railroad franchise."

At this point he paused. His jaws set, and his expression became stern, almost fierce, as he added: "The man died in jail of a broken heart, and I .. and I ..." He took a deep breath and continued as though he were reciting an experience which he had heard related of some stranger.

"I was, of course, violently attacked; and it was a period of terrible strain for me. What with anxiety and overwork I began to suffer from insomnia, and that soon produced a bad condition of my nerves. One morning I went down to The World and called for the editorials which were ready for me to go over. I always read every line of editorial copy. When I picked up the sheets I was astonished to find that I could hardly see the writing, let alone read it. I thought it was probably due to indigestion or to some other temporary cause, and said nothing about it. The next morning on my way downtown I called in at an oculist's. He examined my eyes and then told me to go home and remain in bed in a darkened room for six weeks. At the end of that time he examined me again, said that I had ruptured a blood vessel in one of my eyes, and ordered me to stop work entirely and to take six months' rest in California.

"That was the beginning of the end. Whatever my trouble had been at first, it developed into separation of the retina in both eyes. From the day on which I first consulted the oculist up to the present time, about twenty-four years, I have only been three times in The World building. Most people think I'm dead, or living in Europe in complete retirement. Now go on and give me the morning's news. I've had practically nothing, so you can just run over it briefly, item by item."

On another occasion he told me an amusing story of an experience he had had out in Missouri just after the end of the Civil War. He had spent some weeks riding from county-seat to county-seat securing registration for a deed making title for a railroad. One evening he was nearly drowned through his horse stumbling in the middle of a ford. When he dragged himself up the bank on the other side, drenched to the skin and worried by the prospect of having to catch his mount, which had started off on a cross-country gallop, he saw an elderly farmer sitting on a tree stump, and watching him with intense interest and perfect seriousness.

This man put J. P. up for the night. They got along famously for a while, but presently all was changed.

"The first thing he did," said J. P., "was to take me to the farmhouse and hand me a tumbler three parts full of whisky. When I refused this he looked at me as though he thought I was mad. 'Yer mean ter tell me yer don't drink?' he said. (It was one of the rare occasions when I heard Mr. Pulitzer try to imitate any one's peculiarities of speech.) When I told him no, I didn't, he said nothing, but brought me food.

"After I had eaten he pulled out a plug of tobacco, bit off a large piece, and offered the plug to me. I thanked him, but declined. It took him some time to get over that, but at last he said: 'Yer mean ter tell me yer don't chew?' I said no, I didn't. He dropped the subject, and for an hour or so we talked about the war and the crops and the proposed railroad.

"That man was a gentleman. He didn't take another drink or another chew of tobacco all that time. The only sign he gave of his embarrassment was that every now and then during a pause in the conversation he fell to shaking his head in a puzzled sort of way. Finally, before he went to bed, he produced a pipe, filled it, and handed the tobacco to me; but I failed him again, and he put his own pipe back in his pocket, firmly but sorrowfully.

"Well, my God! it was nearly half an hour before he spoke again, and I was beginning to think that I had really wounded his feelings by declining his hospitable offers, when he came over and stood in front of me and looked down on me with an expression of profound pity. I shall never forget his words. 'Young feller,' he said, 'you seem to be right smart and able for a furriner, but let me tell YOU, you'll never make a successful American until yer learn to drink, and chew, and smoke.'"

Chatwold being within telephone distance of New York, J. P. was constantly subjected to the temptation of ringing up The World in order to discuss editorial or business matters. He yielded too often, and the additional excitement and work incident to these conversations (which were always carried on through a third person) were a severe strain on his vitality. When he was absolutely worn out he would take refuge on the yacht and steam out to sea for the purpose of enjoying a few days of comparative rest.

There is a matter which I may mention in connection with J. P.'s life on the yacht which, trivial as it seems when told at this distance of time, never failed to make a profound impression upon me. Of all the trying moments which were inseparable from attendance upon a blind man with a will of iron and a nervous system of gossamer, no moment was quite so full of uneasiness as that in which J. P. used the gangway in boarding or in leaving the yacht.

Take the case of his going ashore. The yacht lies at anchor in a gentle swell; the launch comes up to the gangway; two or three men with boat-hooks occupy themselves in trying to keep it steady. First over the side goes Dunningham, backward, then Mr. Pulitzer facing forward, one hand on the gang-rail, the other on Dunningham's shoulder; then an officer and one of the secretaries, close behind J. P. and ready to clutch him if he slipped.

Dunningham reaches the grating at the foot of the gangway, then J. P., then there is a pause while the latter is placed in the exact position where one step forward will carry him into the launch, where the officer in charge is ready to receive him.

In the meantime the launch is bobbing up and down, its gunwale at one instant level with the gangway-grating, at another, two or three feet below it. At the precise moment when the launch is almost at the top of its rise Dunningham says: "Now, step, please, Mr. Pulitzer." But J. P. waits just long enough to allow the launch to drop a couple of feet, and then suddenly makes up his mind and tries to step off onto nothing. Dunningham, the officer and the secretary seize him as he cries: "My God! What's the matter? You told me to step."

Then follows a long argument as to what Dunningham had meant precisely when he said "Step!" This whole process might be repeated several times before he actually found himself in the launch.

The whole thing inspired me with a morbid curiosity; and whenever J. P. was going up or down the gangway I always found myself, in common, I may add, with a considerable proportion of the ship's company, leaning over the side watching this nerve-racking exhibition.

I have said that it was J. P.'s custom to seek repose on the yacht when he was worn out with overwork; but it would be more accurate to say that rest was the seldom realized object of these short cruises, for nothing was more difficult for J. P. than to drop his work so long as he had a vestige of strength left with which he could flog his mind into action.

Starting out with the best intentions, J. P.'s cruises of recuperation were usually cut short by putting in to Portland, or New London, or Marblehead to get newspapers and to send telegrams summoning to the yacht one or another of the higher staff of The World.

It was, however, when we anchored, as we often did, off Greenwich, Conn., that J. P. indulged himself to his utmost capacity in conferences with editors and business managers of The World and with one or two outsiders. We would drop anchor in the afternoon, pick up a visitor, cruise in the Sound for a night and a morning, drop anchor again, send the visitor ashore, and pick up another.

Toward the latter part of September, 1911, J. P. left the yacht and moved into his town house in East 73d Street. It was a large and beautifully designed mansion, differing in three particulars from the ordinary run of residences which have been built, furnished, and decorated with the utmost good taste and without regard to expense.

The room in which J. P. usually took his meals was a small but beautifully proportioned retreat so placed that it was completely surrounded by other rooms and had no direct contact with the outside world. It was in its ground plan an irregular octagon, and it drew its light and air from a glass dome. The most striking element in the decorations was a number of slender columns of pale-green Irish marble, which rose from the floor to the dome.

Another unusual feature of the house was a superb church organ, which was built into a large recess halfway up the main staircase. J. P. was an enthusiastic lover of organ music, and heard as much of it as he could during his brief visits to New York.

There are no doubt other houses which have an octagonal dining-room and a church organ; but no other house, I am sure, has a bedroom like that which Mr. Pulitzer occupied. Although it appeared to form part of the house, it did not, in fact, do so. It stood upon its own foundations and was connected with the main structure by some ingenious device which isolated it from all vibrations originating there. It was of the most solid construction, and had but one window, a very large affair, consisting of three casements set one inside the other and provided with heavy plate glass panels. This triple window was never opened when Mr. Pulitzer was in the room, the ventilation being secured by means of fans situated in a long masonry shaft whose interior opening was in the chimney and whose exterior opening was far enough away to forbid the passage of any sound from the street. At intervals inside this shaft were placed frames with silk threads drawn across them, for the purpose of absorbing any faint vibrations which might find their way in. In this bedroom, with its triple window and its heavy double-door closed, J. P. enjoyed as near an approach to perfect quietness as it was possible to attain in New York.

I saw very little of J. P. when he was in New York. He was much occupied with family affairs; he was in constant touch with the staff of The World; and the deep interest he took in the prospects of the presidential election of 1912, which was already being eagerly discussed, brought an unusual number of visitors to the house.

The extent of my intercourse with J. P. at this time was an occasional drive in Central Park, during which we talked of little else but politics, and on that topic of little else but Mr. Woodrow Wilson's speeches and plans.

It did not take very long before the hard work and the excitement of the New York life reduced Mr. Pulitzer to a condition in which it was imperative that he should go to sea again and abandon completely his contact with the daily events which stimulated rather than nourished his mental powers.

On October 20, 1911, the Liberty left New York with J. P., his youngest son, Herbert, and the usual staff. We headed south, with nothing settled as to our plans except that we might spend some time at Mr. Pulitzer's house on Jekyll Island, Ga., and might pass part of the winter cruising in the West Indies.

As soon as we got settled down on board I was delighted to find that J. P. had apparently satisfied himself in regard to my qualifications and limitations. He abandoned the searching examinations which had kept me on the rack for nearly eight months, and our relations became much more agreeable.

Apart from bearing my share in the routine work of dealing with the news of the day and with the current magazine literature my principal duty gradually assumed the form of furnishing humor on demand.

The easiest part of this task was that of reading humorous books to J. P. When he was in the right mood and would submit to the process, I read to him the greater part of "Dooley," of Artemus Ward, of Max Adler, and portions of W. W. Jacobs, of Lorimer's Letters of a Self-made Merchant to His Son, of Mrs. Anne Warner's Susan Clegg and Her Friend Mrs. Lathrop, and of some of Stockton's delightful stories. My greatest triumph was in inducing him to forget for a while his intense aversion to slang and to listen to the shrewd and genial philosophy of George Ade.

The work of the official humorist to J. P. was rendered particularly arduous because he carried into the field of humor, absolutely unabated, his passion for facts. To most people a large part of humor consists in the manner of presentation, in the trick of phrase, in the texture of the narrative. To J. P. those things meant little or nothing; what amused him was the situation disclosed, the inherent humor of the action or thought.

As I have said, it was not difficult to read humorous material to J. P. when he deliberately resigned himself to it. What was exceedingly difficult was to rise to those frequent occasions when, tired, vexed and out of sorts, he suddenly interrupted your summary of a magazine article by saying: "Stop! Stop! For God's sake! I've got a frightful headache. Now tell me some humorous stories - make me laugh."

In order to meet these urgent and embarrassing demands I ransacked the periodical press of England and America. I procured a year's file of Pearson's Weekly, of Tit Bits and of Life, and scores of stray copies of Puck, Judge and Answers.

From these I cut hundreds of short humorous paragraphs, which I kept in a box in my cabin. Whenever I was summoned to attend upon J. P. I put a handful of these clippings in my pocket. I am afraid I should make enemies if I were to tell of the thousands of stories I had to read in order to get the hundreds which came within range even of my modest hopes; but I may say that line for line I got more available stories from the "Newspaper Waifs" on the editorial page of the New York Evening Post than from any other source.

Even after I had labored long and heroically in the vineyard of professional humor, grape juice, and not wine, was the commoner product of my efforts.

It was no unusual experience that after I had told J. P. one of the best tales in my collection he would say: "Well, go on, go on, come to the point. For God's sake, isn't there any end to this story?"

On October 25, 1911, we put into the harbor of Charlestown, S. C. There was the usual business of collecting mail, newspapers, and so on, for J. P., after five days at sea, was eager to pick up the thread of current happenings.

On the following day Mr. Lathan, editor of the Charleston Courier, lunched on the yacht. He and Mr. Pulitzer had an animated discussion about the possibilities of a Democratic victory in 1912. I had never seen J. P. in a more genial mood or in higher spirits.

Whether it was due to the excitement of receiving a visitor whose conversation was so stimulating I do not know; but on Friday, October 27, J. P. was feeling so much out of sorts that he did not appear on deck. On Saturday he remained below only because Dunningham, who always kept the closest watch over his health, persuaded him to have a good rest before resuming the ordinary routine. J. P. was anxious to take up some business matters with Thwaites, but Dunningham induced him to give up the idea.

At three o'clock in the morning of Sunday, October 29, Dunningham came to my cabin and, without making any explanation, said:

"Mr, Pulitzer wishes you to come and read to him."

I put on a dressing gown, gathered up half a dozen books, and in five minutes I was sitting by Mr. Pulitzer's bedside. He was evidently suffering a good deal of pain, for he turned from side to side, and once or twice got out of bed and sat in an easy chair.

I tried several books, but finally settled down to read Macaulay's Essay on Hallam. I read steadily until about five o'clock, and J. P. listened attentively, interrupting me from time to time with a direction to go back and read over a passage.

About half-past five he began to suffer severely, and he sent for the yacht's doctor, who did what was possible for him. At a few minutes after six J. P. said: "Now, Mr. Ireland, you'd better go and get some sleep; we will finish that this afternoon. Good-bye, I'm much obliged to you. Ask Mr. Mann to come to me. Go, now, and have a good rest, and forget all about me."

I slept till noon. When I came on deck I found that everything was going on much as usual. One of the secretaries was with J. P.; the others were at work over the day's papers.

At lunch we spoke of J. P. One man said that he seemed a little worse than usual, another that he had seen him much worse a score of times.

Suddenly the massive door at the forward end of the saloon opened. I turned in my seat and saw framed in the doorway the towering figure of the head butler. I faced his impassive glance, and received the full shock of his calm but incredible announcement: "Mr. Pulitzer is dead."

Choose from Thousands of 1stWorldLibrary Classics By

A. M. Barnard	C. M. Ingleby	Elizabeth Gaskell
Ada Leverson	Carolyn Wells	Elizabeth McCracken
Adolphus William Ward	Catherine Parr Traill	Elizabeth Von Arnim
Aesop	Charles A. Eastman	Ellem Key
Agatha Christie	Charles Amory Beach	Emerson Hough
Alexander Aaronsohn	Charles Dickens	Emilie F. Carlen
Alexander Kielland	Charles Dudley Warner	Emily Dickinson
Alexandre Dumas	Charles Farrar Browne	Enid Bagnold
Alfred Gatty	Charles Ives	Enilor Macartney Lane
Alfred Ollivant	Charles Kingsley	Erasmus W. Jones
Alice Duer Miller	Charles Klein	Ernie Howard Pie
Alice Turner Curtis	Charles Hanson Towne	Ethel May Dell
Alice Dunbar	Charles Lathrop Pack	Ethel Turner
Allen Chapman	Charles Romyn Dake	Ethel Watts Mumford
Ambrose Bierce	Charles Whibley	Eugenie Foa
Amelia E. Barr	Charles Willing Beale	Eugene Wood
Amory H. Bradford	Charlotte M. Braeme	Eustace Hale Ball
Andrew Lang	Charlotte M. Yonge	Evelyn Everett-green
Andrew McFarland Davis	Charlotte Perkins Stetson	Everard Cotes
Andy Adams	Clair W. Hayes	F. H. Cheley
Anna Alice Chapin	Clarence Day Jr.	F. J. Cross
Anna Sewell	Clarence E. Mulford	F. Marion Crawford
Annie Besant	Clemence Housman	Federick Austin Ogg
Annie Hamilton Donnell	Confucius	Ferdinand Ossendowski
Annie Payson Call	Coningsby Dawson	Francis Bacon
Annie Roe Carr	Cornelis DeWitt Wilcox	Francis Darwin
Annonaymous	Cyril Burleigh	Frances Hodgson Burnett
Anton Chekhov	D. H. Lawrence	Frances Parkinson Keyes
Arnold Bennett	Daniel Defoe	Frank Gee Patchin
Arthur Conan Doyle	David Garnett	Frank Harris
Arthur M. Winfield	Dinah Craik	Frank Jewett Mather
Arthur Ransome	Don Carlos Janes	Frank L. Packard
Arthur Schnitzler	Donald Keyhoe	Frank V. Webster
Atticus	Dorothy Kilner	Frederic Stewart Isham
B.H. Baden-Powell	Dougan Clark	Frederick Trevor Hill
B. M. Bower	Douglas Fairbanks	Frederick Winslow Taylor
B. C. Chatterjee	E. Nesbit	Friedrich Kerst
Baroness Emmuska Orczy	E.P.Roe	Friedrich Nietzsche
Baroness Orczy	E. Phillips Oppenheim	Fyodor Dostoyevsky
Basil King	Earl Barnes	G.A. Henty
Bayard Taylor	Edgar Rice Burroughs	G.K. Chesterton
Ben Macomber	Edith Van Dyne	Gabrielle E. Jackson
Bertha Muzzy Bower	Edith Wharton	Garrett P. Serviss
Bjornstjerne Bjornson	Edward Everett Hale	Gaston Leroux
Booth Tarkington	Edward J. O'Biren	George A. Warren
Boyd Cable	Edward S. Ellis	George Ade
Bram Stoker	Edwin L. Arnold	Geroge Bernard Shaw
C. Collodi	Eleanor Atkins	George Durston
C. E. Orr	Eliot Gregory	George Ebers

George Eliot
George Gissing
George MacDonald
George Meredith
George Orwell
George Sylvester Viereck
George Tucker
George W. Cable
George Wharton James
Gertrude Atherton
Gordon Casserly
Grace E. King
Grace Gallatin
Grace Greenwood
Grant Allen
Guillermo A. Sherwell
Gulielma Zollinger
Gustav Flaubert
H. A. Cody
H. B. Irving
H.C. Bailey
H. G. Wells
H. H. Munro
H. Irving Hancock
H. Rider Haggard
H. W. C. Davis
Haldeman Julius
Hall Caine
Hamilton Wright Mabie
Hans Christian Andersen
Harold Avery
Harold McGrath
Harriet Beecher Stowe
Harry Castlemon
Harry Coghill
Harry Houidini
Hayden Carruth
Helent Hunt Jackson
Helen Nicolay
Hendrik Conscience
Hendy David Thoreau
Henri Barbusse
Henrik Ibsen
Henry Adams
Henry Ford
Henry Frost
Henry James
Henry Jones Ford
Henry Seton Merriman
Henry W Longfellow
Herbert A. Giles

Herbert Carter
Herbert N. Casson
Herman Hesse
Hildegard G. Frey
Homer
Honore De Balzac
Horace B. Day
Horace Walpole
Horatio Alger Jr.
Howard Pyle
Howard R. Garis
Hugh Lofting
Hugh Walpole
Humphry Ward
Ian Maclaren
Inez Haynes Gillmore
Irving Bacheller
Isabel Hornibrook
Israel Abrahams
Ivan Turgenev
J.G.Austin
J. Henri Fabre
J. M. Barrie
J. Macdonald Oxley
J. S. Fletcher
J. S. Knowles
J. Storer Clouston
Jack London
Jacob Abbott
James Allen
James Andrews
James Baldwin
James Branch Cabell
James DeMille
James Joyce
James Lane Allen
James Lane Allen
James Oliver Curwood
James Oppenheim
James Otis
James R. Driscoll
Jane Austen
Jane L. Stewart
Janet Aldridge
Jens Peter Jacobsen
Jerome K. Jerome
John Burroughs
John Cournos
John F. Kennedy
John Gay
John Glasworthy

John Habberton
John Joy Bell
John Kendrick Bangs
John Milton
John Philip Sousa
Jonas Lauritz Idemil Lie
Jonathan Swift
Joseph A. Altsheler
Joseph Carey
Joseph Conrad
Joseph E. Badger Jr
Joseph Hergesheimer
Joseph Jacobs
Jules Vernes
Julian Hawthrone
Julie A Lippmann
Justin Huntly McCarthy
Kakuzo Okakura
Kenneth Grahame
Kenneth McGaffey
Kate Langley Bosher
Kate Langley Bosher
Katherine Cecil Thurston
Katherine Stokes
L. A. Abbot
L. T. Meade
L. Frank Baum
Latta Griswold
Laura Dent Crane
Laura Lee Hope
Laurence Housman
Lawrence Beasley
Leo Tolstoy
Leonid Andreyev
Lewis Carroll
Lewis Sperry Chafer
Lilian Bell
Lloyd Osbourne
Louis Hughes
Louis Tracy
Louisa May Alcott
Lucy Fitch Perkins
Lucy Maud Montgomery
Luther Benson
Lydia Miller Middleton
Lyndon Orr
M. Corvus
M. H. Adams
Margaret E. Sangster
Margret Howth
Margaret Vandercook

Margret Penrose
Maria Edgeworth
Maria Thompson Daviess
Mariano Azuela
Marion Polk Angellotti
Mark Overton
Mark Twain
Mary Austin
Mary Catherine Crowley
Mary Cole
Mary Hastings Bradley
Mary Roberts Rinehart
Mary Rowlandson
M. Wollstonecraft Shelley
Maud Lindsay
Max Beerbohm
Myra Kelly
Nathaniel Hawthrone
Nicolo Machiavelli
O. F. Walton
Oscar Wilde
Owen Johnson
P.G. Wodehouse
Paul and Mabel Thorne
Paul G. Tomlinson
Paul Severing
Percy Brebner
Peter B. Kyne
Plato
R. Derby Holmes
R. L. Stevenson
R. S. Ball
Rabindranath Tagore
Rahul Alvares
Ralph Bonehill
Ralph Henry Barbour
Ralph Victor
Ralph Waldo Emmerson
Rene Descartes
Rex Beach

Rex E. Beach
Richard Harding Davis
Richard Jefferies
Richard Le Gallienne
Robert Barr
Robert Frost
Robert Gordon Anderson
Robert L. Drake
Robert Lansing
Robert Lynd
Robert Michael Ballantyne
Robert W. Chambers
Rosa Nouchette Carey
Rudyard Kipling
Samuel B. Allison
Samuel Hopkins Adams
Sarah Bernhardt
Sarah C. Hallowell
Selma Lagerlof
Sherwood Anderson
Sigmund Freud
Standish O'Grady
Stanley Weyman
Stella Benson
Stella M. Francis
Stephen Crane
Stewart Edward White
Stijn Streuvels
Swami Abhedananda
Swami Parmananda
T. S. Ackland
T. S. Arthur
The Princess Der Ling
Thomas A. Janvier
Thomas A Kempis
Thomas Anderton
Thomas Bailey Aldrich
Thomas Bulfinch
Thomas De Quincey
Thomas Dixon

Thomas H. Huxley
Thomas Hardy
Thomas More
Thornton W. Burgess
U. S. Grant
Valentine Williams
Various Authors
Vaughan Kester
Victor Appleton
Victoria Cross
Virginia Woolf
Wadsworth Camp
Walter Camp
Walter Scott
Washington Irving
Wilbur Lawton
Wilkie Collins
Willa Cather
Willard F. Baker
William Dean Howells
William le Queux
W. Makepeace Thackeray
William W. Walter
William Shakespeare
Winston Churchill
Yei Theodora Ozaki
Yogi Ramacharaka
Young E. Allison
Zane Grey

www.ingramcontent.com/pod-product-compliance
Lightning Source LLC
Chambersburg PA
CBHW020505100426
42813CB00030B/3129/J